THE THEORY OF CON

Other books by Rodney Collin, all published by Shambhala:
The Theory of Celestial Influence
The Theory of Eternal Life
The Mirror of Light

THE THEORY OF
Conscious Harmony

From the Letters of
Rodney Collin

SHAMBHALA
Boulder & London 1984

SHAMBHALA PUBLICATIONS, INC.
Boulder, Colorado 80306-0271

9 8 7 6 5 4 3 2 1
First Shambhala edition

Distributed in the United States by Random House
and in Canada by Random House of Canada Ltd.

Library of Congress Cataloging in Publication Data

Collin, Rodney.
The theory of conscious harmony.

Reprint. Originally published: London: Watkins, 1958.
1. Spiritual life—Miscellanea. I. Title.
BF1999.C679 1984 128 84-5494
ISBN 0-87773-285-X (pbk.)
ISBN 0-394-72698-7 (Random House: pbk.)

Cover painting "Borning of Light," by Pepin Hernandez Laos.
Produced by special arrangement with Vista Nueva, Inc., Box 190248,
Dallas, TX 75219

CONTENTS

	page
BIOGRAPHICAL NOTE	vii
BEING	1
CONSCIENCE	15
MANHOOD AND WOMANHOOD	20
KNOWLEDGE	22
UNDERSTANDING	28
IMAGINATION	36
DIFFERENT 'I'S	37
SEPARATION OF THE REAL AND FALSE	39
CONTRADICTIONS	45
ACCEPTANCE	47
POSITIVE ATTITUDE	52
INVISIBILITY	58
ATTENTION	60
REQUIREMENTS AND CIRCUMSTANCES	64
SELF-REMEMBERING	70
OTHER PEOPLE	72
CORRECTING MISTAKES	81
THE INFLUENCE OF CONSCIOUS MEN	84
TIME	89
HEART	95
PRAYER	98
HIGHER STATES	100
BODY, SOUL AND SPIRIT	104
TRACES OF SCHOOL	109
DIFFERENT WAYS	118
RELIGION	123
HIERARCHY	130
HARMONY	137
THE WORK	143
KAIROS, CHRONOS AND CROSSROADS	166
SUFFERING	169
DEATH	176
THE NEW BEGINNING	179
CUZCO	187
QUESTIONNAIRE	189
EXPLANATORY NOTES	195
PUBLISHED WORKS	212

BIOGRAPHICAL NOTE

RODNEY COLLIN SMITH was born in Brighton, England, on April 26, 1909. His father was a general merchant who retired from his business in London at the age of fifty, as had always been his intention, and after a journey to the continent and Egypt, settled in Brighton and married Kathleen Logan, the daughter of a hotel proprietor. They lived in a comfortable house on Brighton Front, where Rodney was born. His brother was born four years later.

His mother was interested in astrology and belonged to the local Theosophical Lodge. She spent much of her time transcribing books into Braille for the blind.

Rodney went first to Brighton College Preparatory School (a nearby day-school), then as a boarder to Ashford Grammar School in Kent. He spent his holidays reading, usually a book a day which he got from the public library, and walking and exploring the neighbouring countryside. On leaving school he spent three years at the London School of Economics, living at the Toc H hostel in Fitzroy Square.

In 1926 he spent the summer holidays with a French family in the Chateaux country, and from then on went every year to the continent. At eighteen he went to Spain, provided by his parents with money calculated to last for a month. By living in inns and farmhouses and in the cheapest hotels and walking much of the way he managed to tour Andalusia for three months, returning with voluminous notes which formed the material for *Palms and Patios*, a book of essays published by Heath Cranton in 1931. During this trip he learned enough Spanish to cause his being drafted into the censorship during the war and greatly to facilitate his orientation in Mexico in 1948.

On leaving the London School of Economics where he had taken his B.Com., he earned his living by free-lance journalism on art and travel, contributing also a series of weekly articles to the *Evening Standard* and *Sunday Referee* on weekend walks round London. For a time he was secretary of the Youth

Hostels Association, editor of their journal *The Rucsack*, and assistant editor of the *Toc H Journal.*

In 1929 he visited Austria, Hungary and Czechoslovakia. On a pilgrimage organised by Toc H to the Passion Play in Oberammergau in 1930 he met Janet Buckley, his future wife. In the same year he read *A New Model of the Universe* by P. D. Ouspensky. He felt that he was not ready for it yet, but that it would be very important for him later.

In the autumn of 1931 he went on a walking-tour through Dalmatia, later describing some of his adventures there in two articles that appeared in the *Cornhill Magazine.*

He and his wife were married in London in March 1934, and spent their honeymoon walking in Cornwall. Later in the year they spent six weeks in Sicily. In 1935 they were introduced to some lectures given by Dr Maurice Nicoll, but shortly after left for a six-months' motor journey through the United States to the west coast, returning along the Mexican border.

In the autumn of 1936 he and his wife first met Mr Ouspensky. Rodney immediately recognised that he had found what he had been searching for in his reading and travels. From then on he dedicated all his time to the study of Mr Ouspensky's teaching.

His daughter Chloe was born in 1937. He and his family moved to a house in Virginia Water near Lyne Place, which Mr and Madame Ouspensky had taken as a centre for their work. When not at Lyne Rodney spent much of his time in the British Museum Library studying those aspects of religion, philosophy, science and art which seemed most immediately connected with Mr Ouspensky's lectures. That year he and his wife went on a short holiday to Roumania and later for a two-weeks motor trip through Algeria to the north of the Sahara.

In 1938 he took part in a demonstration in London of the movements and dances which formed part of the system taught by Mr Ouspensky, and immediately afterwards went to Syria in the hopes of seeing the 'turning' of the Mevlevi Dervishes. This he was unable to do, though he met the sheikh of the tekye in Damascus.

On the outbreak of war he and his family moved to Lyne

Place. Shortly after, his wife and daughter went to the United States to help prepare a house in New Jersey for Mr and Madame Ouspensky, who planned to move there within a few months. Rodney remained at Lyne, working in London in the censorship during the day and in the local air raid defence at night. In February 1941 he was transferred to Bermuda, by coincidence on the same ship on which Mr Ouspensky travelled to the United States, to which Madame Ouspensky had gone a few weeks previously.

After six months in Bermuda Rodney joined the British Security organisation in New York. For the next six years he and his family lived at Franklin Farms, Mendham, a large house with gardens and farm where work was organised for the English families who had joined Mr and Madame Ouspensky and numerous others who attended Mr Ouspensky's lectures in New York. Rodney commuted to and from his office by train every day and spent the evenings and weekends on the farm.

In 1943, he was sent to Canada on official business. In 1943, 1944 and 1945 he spent his short leaves from duty in Mexico, to which country he was strongly attracted. When war ended he left British Government service and devoted himself entirely to the work of Mr and Madame Ouspensky.

Gradually, however, he spent more and more time with Mr Ouspensky, driving him to and from New York for his meetings and usually spending the evening with him at a restaurant or in his study at Franklin Farms. He became deeply attached to Mr Ouspensky in a way that included, without being limited by, personal affection and respect. While formerly he had concentrated on Mr Ouspensky's teaching, it was now the teacher and what he was demonstrating which occupied Rodney's attention.

Mr Ouspensky returned to England in the early spring of 1947. Rodney left Mendham just before Easter, spending a week in Paris before joining Mr Ouspensky at Lyne Place. He was with him constantly all summer and autumn until Mr Ouspensky's death on October 2, 1947.

The experiences that Rodney went through at this time profoundly affected his whole being. During the week following

Mr Ouspensky's death he reached a perception of what his future work was to be. He realised that, while attached to his teacher for and through all time, he must reconstruct in himself what Mr Ouspensky had given him and thereafter take the responsibility of expressing it according to his own understanding.

He moved to London, where he and his wife lived quietly for the next six months. During the previous summer he had begun *The Theory of Celestial Influence*, and finished it in the spring of 1948. Many people came to see him at his flat in St. James's Street, where weekly meetings were held, attended by a number of the people who had worked with Mr Ouspensky, some of whom were to join him later in Mexico.

In June 1948 he and a small party left for New York en route for Mexico, which he felt was his place for a new beginning.

They spent six months in Guadalajara. Here Rodney finished *The Theory of Eternal Life*, which he had begun in London, and wrote *Hellas*, a play. Then they moved to Mexico City and after a few months took a large house in Tlalpam, where they were joined by a number of friends, many from England. Meetings were started in a flat taken for the purpose in Mexico City and attended by a number of Mexicans and people of other nationalities. For a time there were meetings in both English and Spanish, until those of the English-speaking group who remained had learned sufficient Spanish to participate in joint meetings conducted in the latter language. The nucleus of a permanent group was gradually formed.

In the spring of 1949 the first translations into Spanish of Mr Ouspensky's books were begun. These were subsequently published by Ediciones Sol, which Rodney formed for the purpose. During the following years some fourteen titles were published, which included books by Dr Nicoll, Rodney himself, and several others connected with the Work. A number of booklets were also published on different religious traditions which Rodney felt to be expressions of related ideas.

One of the chief plans which Rodney had visualised during the week after Mr Ouspensky's death was for a three-dimensional diagram expressing simultaneously the many cosmic laws which were the basis of their studies—a building through which people could move and feel its meaning. In 1949 a site in the mountains behind Mexico City was acquired and in 1951 the foundation stone of what is now known as the Planetarium of Tetecala was laid. Tetecala means 'Stone House of God' in Aztec, and happened to be the name of the field in which it is situated. This building became the focal point of Rodney's work with his people during the subsequent years.

In the spring of 1954 it was decided to leave the house at Tlalpam. Twelve public performances of Ibsen's *Peer Gynt* were given in the garden as a demonstration of group work, under the name of the Unicorn Players. Rodney played the part of the Button Moulder. Later that year, those who had lived at Tlalpam moved to individual homes in Mexico City.

In 1954 and 1955 Rodney made journeys to Europe and the Near East, the basic reason for which was to collect material of and make connections with esoteric schools of the past. On his visit to Rome in 1954 he was received into the Roman Catholic Church, a step which he had been contemplating for some time.

As a consequence of the distribution of the Ediciones Sol books in Latin America groups were started in Peru, Chile, the Argentine and Uruguay, and contacts made in several other countries on the American continent. In January 1955 Rodney visited the groups in Lima and Buenos Aires and went to Cuzco and Maccu Picchu to study the remains of their ancient civilisations.

In the autumn of 1955 the Unicorn Players produced *The Lark*, a play by Jean Anouilh about Joan of Arc, in which Rodney played Bishop Cauchon.

In January 1956 he led an all-night pilgrimage on foot from the Planetarium to the shrine of Our Lady of Guadalupe, some 30 miles. During Mass in the Basilica he apparently fainted from exhaustion, though later it seemed evident that this was the first of a series of heart attacks from which he died in Peru on May 3, 1956. An account of his death will be found at the end of this book.

These quotations have been edited to the extent of omitting names and references to personal situations. Occasionally two or three letters that contained similar phrases have been condensed into one; also sometimes the wording has been changed from 'you' to 'we'—'I think you should' to 'it seems that we should'. Otherwise the quotations have been taken direct from the carbon copies my husband kept of almost all his letters between 1944 and 1956. Nothing has been added and no dates changed.

Janet Collin Smith

Words marked with an asterisk are explained in the Notes on page 195

BEING

August 4, 1944 'Constantly perform action which is duty . . .' (Bhagavad Gita)—this seems to be the way out of the impasse where man's impulses and personal ambitions constantly push him into activities which still further feed these same ambitions and impulses.

But it is one thing to see this as a clear idea, another to live by it. So much so, that sometimes one is forced to put aside all that one has read in books or heard, and ask oneself what one really knows for oneself, knows in such a way that all one's conduct is guided by it.

March 14, 1947 We pass through certain phases, come to certain problems, that can only be solved by ourselves. The only help that is possible is when other people are friendly and open-hearted and patient, even though we may make it very difficult for them to be so. I doubt whether any other kind is possible on our level.

There are many things we have accepted in theory; but we have not yet seen their full implications. The mind is very slick; it has the blueprints and can describe them. But the being of man is a jungle, as the Mathnawi says, and there are many creatures there that we have not yet assessed, have not tamed. There are so many possibilities, for good or evil, that we have not yet seen. So much is unknown when we look into ourselves, our fate, our duty, our connections with people and things around us. We are like men who have studied the theory and history of architecture, but haven't yet started building their own houses.

It is the individual himself who in the end has to get in there and do the work, if he is to reap the harvest he wants. No one else can do the work for him, no one else can solve his problems, no one can persuade him or coax him. He must find something in himself that longs above everything to grow, to struggle, to wake up. Then he may be some use perhaps, not otherwise. This is how it seems.

JULY 25, 1948 If people always remember that they cannot lose by experiment, *they can only lose by trying nothing*, much can be learned. Much can *always* be learned; good times or bad times—it is all the same from one point of view.

NOVEMBER 5, 1949 There is a phase when one has to go away from external knowledge, and find everything in oneself.

NOVEMBER 27, 1949 It is not necessary to give up one's own point of view easily, nor to agree with other people just because one likes them. From my point of view, what makes the work of a group much more interesting than that of an individual, is that each person should find in himself his own sincere viewpoint, which is peculiarly his, and contribute it to the whole—in this way the whole becomes rich and balanced.

AUGUST 30, 1950 The reason why some people do not understand each other is quite simply because they are at different points on a circle. It is not necessary that the different points should agree, and follow a middle course. On the contrary, each point must fulfil its own duty as purely as possible, without imitating the duty of another, which has nothing to do with it. How awful if we were all Collin Smiths or X's! All that is necessary to attain tranquillity in our differences is to learn to understand the great whole, the majesty of the great plan in which each has a part. From there one begins to respect the duties of others without wanting to change them.

NOVEMBER 24, 1950 What you know, you know. Do not let anyone steal that from you, with the best intentions.

FEBRUARY 15, 1951 We can regard impressions as all that which enters from the outside world through the five senses. Only these impressions may just reach us without affecting us internally in any way, or they may enter us very deeply, their innermost meaning may be seen, and they may become transformed into intense emotion. For instance, one walks on the street and receives an impression of a beggar—one day it will be just a vague face which one takes as part of the scenery and which has no more significance for one than an old piece of newspaper. Another day one may actually *see* the man, see all he has been through, see what he is, see all that he can expect to become. Such a perception may suddenly connect with many pictures, memories and experiences, and give a flash of new understanding. It need not be a beggar. The same thing can happen through the simplest scene or object. The impression may be the same that one receives every day, but one day it is *digested*, that is, transformed into higher hydrogen*. And this transformation is directly or indirectly connected with the possibility of self-remembering*. Such moments may come as a result of efforts to self-remember; and they may in turn make a new level of self-remembering possible.

In the chapter on 'Experimental Mysticism' in *A New Model* it is described how in certain mystical states 'what is ordinarily objective becomes subjective, and what is ordinarily subjective becomes objective'. In self-remembering, one takes the first step towards this, and it may happen that inner voices, arguments, thoughts, emotions, hopes, fears, aspirations, which in the ordinary way are felt as subjective, as 'I' and 'mine', suddenly become objective, become 'he' and 'his'. In this way one begins to find different people within one. One's own inner life becomes the object of observation, gives one new and important impressions. And one comes to perhaps the deepest question of all, 'Who am I?'

June 20, 1951 Energy and will and effort can be useful. Only sometimes something has to melt first, otherwise it is will, will, will for its own sake, like beating one's head on a wall.

Some people seem to play the part of one who has to walk a long difficult way home. They plod, plod, put one foot in front of the other, until at last the sense of muscular effort, of making themselves go on, seems the only thing in the world. Finally they come opposite their house. They have only to turn in and enter. But they do not notice, because the effort of plodding has become so inevitable that they can't imagine anything else. So they keep right on going, on, on, on to nowhere.

A miracle* was done which brought certain things *actually*

within our reach now. I think that the belief that these things can only be achieved with tremendous effort and self-mortification and shame and time, is exactly the illusion that prevents us enjoying them *at once*.

Some people are like men laboriously digging an enormous well to reach water, when a clear stream is flowing past two yards away. In some, pride in effort has to melt, and they have to sit back quietly and let good things gently soak into them, certainty gently spring up in them.

They feel that gentle and pleasant impulses, warmth and humanity, are of the devil and have to be exorcised with effort, 'going against oneself', unpleasantness and discomfort. But my experience over the last years is that it is exactly the impulse towards that which is *both good and pleasant*, that reveals to each person what his true path really is. We cannot be what we are not, do what we are not made for. No school expects it of us. We can only be what we really are, do what we really can—*in a higher service*. And that is pleasure, happiness.

SEPTEMBER 9, 1951 Perhaps finding one's role is connected with finding the positive side of one's weaknesses, and the higher possibilities of one's likes. But to one's own role one must come; then everything else falls into place.

NOVEMBER 12, 1951 How does desire grow? The wider the vision the greater the desire. We desire little because we see little. As we see more, desire grows. If we see enough, it becomes uncontainable.

NOVEMBER 28, 1951 The question of aim is not easy. It is not so much that one 'accepts' any particular aim. For this suggests that there is a choice. There is no choice. My wish is that each person should find what their *real* aim is, what they want. For no aim that isn't real, no imitated aim or wished-for aim is going to move anyone anywhere. So I would rather someone said frankly: 'My aim is to produce a first-class play', than for him to say: 'My aim is to wish to become conscious.' For from the first he can begin to move here and now, whereas he may sit twenty years in the second without any appreciable change at all. My experience is that behind real aims, even apparently material or worldly ones, a man may if he wishes find the deeper desires and possibilities of his essence*. Whereas 'noble aims' often (though not always of course) arise from beautiful imagination of personality* and can find no daily nourishment. It is most clear that those who know certainly what their own immediate first line is, who take full responsibility for it, and willingly overcome all obstacles connected with it, by that very fact make openings for others and create all kinds of possibilities that those who only wish to 'work on themselves', or something subjective like that, never do.

You remember one of Ouspensky's last meetings:

OUSPENSKY: If I know your aim, perhaps I will be able to say something.

QUESTION: How can I find permanent aim?

OUSPENSKY: Find an impermanent aim first. Why do you begin with permanent aim? It is very difficult and very long. How can you find it?

QUESTION: Can one find a permanent aim by seeing one's situation, seeing what one is?

OUSPENSKY: I don't know. Depends what means permanent aim.

QUESTION: An aim stronger than those we ordinarily know in life.

OUSPENSKY: Why are these aims bad? Why cannot they be used? If you cannot find permanent aim, why not begin on impermanent?

MARCH 4, 1952 There is much to do, on a big scale as well as on a small one. And he who already knows his own aim in life most easily finds his place in the Work.

APRIL 2, 1952 It sometimes happens that we interpret complete stagnation as 'liberation'. On this road we can only hope to liberate ourselves from our illusions and limitations, never from struggle, discomfort and responsibility, which, on the contrary, ought to increase with the strength and understanding of the student. There is very much to be done. But fortunately the greater the widening of our vision, the more interesting our work becomes, and the more 'interior food'* we derive from everything and from everyone with whom we come into contact.

MAY 1, 1952 One has to form within oneself one's own judgement of the esoteric. Ouspensky himself always told us: 'You must not believe me. Observe. Prove or disprove what I say. You must come to your own conclusions.'

Easy acceptance on the one hand or negative argument on the other are equally resistant obstacles, each belonging to different types of people.

MAY 20, 1952 I think of essence and personality like this. Let us take the digestion of food. It enters the mouth and passes to the stomach. There it is ground, purified, mixed, warmed and prepared for passing into the bloodstream. But while it is in the stomach it is not yet organically part of the man himself. Only when food is digested into the form of chyme does it enter the bloodstream, is organically absorbed into the man. It is an integral part of him.

We can take the digestion of experience in the same way. It enters by the five senses and passes into personality. There it is ground, purified, mixed, warmed and prepared to enter into essence. But while it is in personality it is not yet organically part of the man himself. It can always be lost. Only when experience is digested in the form of understanding or permanent capacity does it enter into essence and is organically absorbed into the man. It is an integral part of him.

AUGUST 23, 1952 There are tremendous possibilities before us. I say 'possibilities' because although now they present themselves as practical possibilities, they depend on our efforts and our understanding.

A little before his death Ouspensky, after having spent a whole night forcing his dying body to walk, and waking us in order to make many experiments, said to me: 'Now do you understand that everything has to be done by effort, or do you still think that things come right by themselves?' It was difficult to answer sincerely. Because at that moment I saw clearly that if we really understood that everything is done by effort, all our life would be on another basis. We would not be able to *hope*.

It is strange that in these last years, nearly all the nebulous ideas that I had before about esoteric work have presented themselves as practical possibilities—but depending upon my own work and effort. I have understood that we ourselves have to develop our own will up to the highest possible point; that is, the power of putting into practice what we know. It is a duty inherent in the esoteric economy.

AUGUST 28, 1952 In order to find his real field of work, a man has first to find himself. In some superlogical way all types* enjoy all possibilities. Through being themselves they can find everything—at any rate when they are disciples.

OCTOBER 1952 To seek the Kingdom of God always implies willingness to accept many *more* responsibilities, not to avoid those we already bear. Often in the stimulus of new experiences this fact is forgotten.

DECEMBER 15, 1952 I feel that each group must find and adhere to its own inner line, no matter how this may appear to contradict that of others. At the same time I see no reason why this should mean quarrels or disputes, any more than there need be quarrels between the brain, the heart and the liver. In fact the more certain a group is in its own line, it seems to me the more generous and understanding it can afford to be towards others.

JANUARY 19, 1953 Those who have found a profession through which they can learn and apply these ideas are very lucky. This is the most satisfactory situation—that one can make of one's profession one's own way. Because it is characteristic of the tradition we are studying that it must be realised in life itself. Of course its realisation through one's profession is not a question of months nor of years but of a whole lifetime. But to have a profession that harmonises with one's aim is already an enormous advantage.

AUGUST 29, 1953 Although it may be necessary for a certain length of time for a person to give up his own line of work and interest, in order to rediscover it on another scale, I am quite sure that in the long run each person has to find his way and his contribution through what most deeply satisfies him. The work eventually uses us for what we are, not for what we are not. All the rest is preparation. It would surely be very bad economics if the Great Work used a chisel as a screwdriver and an architect's square as a paper-knife!

Certainly there is more to it than this. For a man's feature (or talent as the Gospels say) can be either his undoing or his salvation. If it is at the service of personality, it will be his weakness, that which trips him up. But if the same thing serves essence or an ideal then it is that which justifies the man's existence in the world, which enables him to fulfil himself and to serve the Work.

SEPTEMBER 24, 1953 Nobody can or should supplant one's own inner way of understanding. I have always been convinced that each person has his own potential way of responding to school* direction. With some people this response takes 'psychic' forms, with others it may take the form of logical understanding, a flair for right action, healing, art. God knows what. When a group becomes organic, all these individual responses dovetail together and reveal the plan being manifested.

No one is expected to have faith in what they have not experienced. Faith is never to go back on what one has already known at certain times *oneself*. This is the only way to the miraculous. And if the miraculous comes as a result of it, let it come!

FEBRUARY 25, 1954 We must not hanker after what our companions *were*. That does not help them or us or the Work. We must long for what they will be, and what we will be.

SEPTEMBER 1, 1954 One has to learn to be. There is no substitute. I think each person has to find his own way of returning to the state of complete certainty and freedom—it may be by meditating alone in silence, by praying, by music, by certain reading or pictures, or in the happy affection of chosen companions. Anyway, when we expect to find ourselves in critical circumstances, we must first restore this freedom in ourselves, and then project it intentionally before consideration and timidity reaches us from others.

SEPTEMBER 1, 1954 It is very clear to me that we are trying to make free people and strong people, who will have confidence enough to act from their own deepest feelings in any circumstances.

SEPTEMBER 20, 1954 Surely what unites all traces of our work is a point of view. I believe the same point of view can be presented in diametrically opposite ways, and often was in the past, in order to make people think for themselves.

SEPTEMBER 20, 1954 We must never forget that nothing that can happen or can be said can affect *what we are*. And it is from *what we are* that we can help others. Difficulties are a test of being. We have to show by example that inner certainty resolves all things.

OCTOBER 19, 1954 Tremendous pressure is being put on people to help them find their own true place, their own inner source of certainty. Whatever happens we must not let ourselves be shaken in what we really know. We need not fight or challenge. But we must never allow our own faith to be sapped, however little it is understood. We must always act and speak from it, never from imitation. This is very important—on a big scale it is important.

NOVEMBER 6, 1954 The first condition of being helped and used by Great School is to find one's *own way*, to have confidence in what one can become. The man who is himself, who is sincere and determined to do what he knows he must, will receive all the help he needs.

FEBRUARY 11, 1955 It's sad if a place which has provided the conditions of movement in one period becomes an inhabited museum the next—and difficult to prevent. It is true that one feels a little lost when the background of work that one has become accustomed to, is taken away. But when one exposes oneself without this background, in no time at all life begins to demand new expressions of work from one, new experiments, new solutions. Everything begins to move again. I don't say it's comfortable, but it's lively.

It is important to take work in new conditions as a *new way of working*, not repetition of the old way. Work is never work if it doesn't progress. It has to progress by mutual understanding, real love, harmony. It progresses by leaving fears behind. Fear of losing old forms, fear of being left naked, fear of opinions, fear of the new, fear of the forces of life—all these must be left behind. To understand the big work, we must be free of all fear whatsoever.

This Work is in each of us, in ourselves. It means making a permanent certainty within ourselves out of what we have received. Then it means projecting this certainty to others around us. We have to give to receive. We have to teach to learn. To teach is to understand, to understand is to accept, to accept is to realise, to realise is to find truth.

FEBRUARY 11, 1955 Really every sincere experiment is wonderful, if one doesn't stop in the middle, but carries it through to the point where it attracts inspiration and high help. Everybody has to find their way to this point individually. Everybody has to find their own way, their own understanding, their alert conscience. They have to accept by themselves for themselves what self-remembering means for them.

FEBRUARY 23, 1955 Everybody has known truth in different degrees—very few people understand that it must be consciously fixed, and nobody but oneself can do the fixing. Higher powers can tint us with their understanding, but we have to take the mordant ourselves.

JULY 18, 1955 About Ouspensky's teaching, it is not only a question of a philosophical system or of a great teacher. It is more like a field of influence which was projected through Gurdjieff and Ouspensky from an invisible level much beyond them. When we really enter this field of influence and expose ourselves to it, many things change for us. Some things become easier, others harder. Some doors close and others open.

Only it takes a very long time and much study and experience to take advantage of this situation. For to do so we have to learn to be ourselves, to find a new confidence and security deep in ourselves. Then we will feel ourselves more and more intimately connected with an influence which is completely reliable, because it does not originate in our world.

August 12, 1955 The only sanity lies in far and high vision. In the light of that, we know we are all fellow-actors, though we don't yet guess our true relationships or even how the plot is going to develop.

All I wish is that we should learn to be sincere and consistent, be really ourselves, not talking in one way and acting in another. Like everybody else, I profess beliefs which I am tempted to forget when living up to them is inconvenient and uncomfortable. To be sincere and consistent in one's own position, whatever it may be—that's not easy. Because personality enters in. I see that our teachers didn't do this. They lived consistently by the pattern of their belief, no matter how unpleasant or how much misunderstood. Were there ever two men who silently absorbed more misunderstanding than Ouspensky and Gurdjieff? But they were strong enough to swallow all that, and go straight on playing their true roles. Perhaps this is the final proof of their greatness.

I don't think it matters what position is taken, if it is taken honestly. Each man's conscience gives him an individual credo. But the important thing is to be true and consistent in that credo. Trying to please other people whose credos are different is exhausting, demoralising and leads nowhere. I wish we could give it up and become free in our differences. For that is harmony. And that is what I am after.

October 3, 1955 Of course we must never give up the expression of our talents. They are God-given gifts. What shall we do if we throw away the possibilities which God has given us to fulfil our individual tasks?

OCTOBER 22, 1955 I think one's own work is much simpler than we imagine. It is the constant effort to become honest, truthful and sincere. Honest—realising that everything has to be paid for, both what one wants for oneself and for others, and to be up to date in one's payment is great happiness and freedom; truthful to measure everything and everybody, including oneself, impartially by the laws we have been given, not by comfort and preferences; sincere—learning to be truly oneself, to make one's *own* way without imitation even of those we admire most. In the field of influence in which we now find ourselves we are being watched and helped all the time. In proportion as we achieve these three qualities, we will also be used.

I feel very much the truth of the parable about the workers in the vineyard—how the ones who came at the first hour, the third, the sixth, all received the same payment. It is the same now with groups all over the world. The same higher help is available to them, no matter whether they have been working twenty years, or five, or one.

NOVEMBER 30, 1955 We must find everything by ourselves in ourselves, without stumbling over words, but feel the meaning of everything within ourselves.

The key of our work is to give; to give we must have, to have we first have to find. We have to find who is ourself, who he was and who he ought to be. Then be it.

DECEMBER 22, 1955 Why should we be afraid when we find ourselves saying more than we know? That must happen to us, if we are to become useful instruments. Some have written like that, some have painted like that, some have simply acted like that. Then we must understand the meaning of what has been said or written or acted through us. And so we grow and make it really our own.

DECEMBER 26, 1955 We must all—both as groups and individuals—find our different ways of understanding and manifesting the great truth which is above us as best we can. If we all used the same way of expressing that truth, we should be merely repeating each other, and how dull that would be for those who are directing us!

Fortunately, the influence under which we live seems to be pressing us all every day harder to be our true selves, to leave behind pretensions and protections, and to affirm what we know clearly and bravely. It is made so extraordinarily uncomfortable to loiter that we have every possible incentive to go on towards light and freedom.

FEBRUARY 2, 1956 What strange things happen to us, when we are alert. Fate pushes us into a corner, and if we don't try to slip out from under, teaches us as much in minutes as would otherwise take years to learn. But what is this fate which knocks the ground from under our feet precisely that we should learn to fly? And who arranges it? That we must find out.

As one goes on, if one is on the right road, it will happen more and more. Sometimes disconcerting, sometimes unbearable—but those moments when we are stripped of habit, and left helpless, are really the moments of our opportunity. It is important not to struggle against them or run away—but quietly go through them to something new.

FEBRUARY 7, 1956 When we speak to people, we must learn more and more to speak in our *own* words, our *own* understanding, without worrying how it sounds, asking them simple sincere questions which they cannot take theoretically. It is impossible to remain theoretical in the face of real simplicity and sincerity. But this means that we have to be very simple, sincere and humble ourselves, speaking without guile and acknowledging what we have found from our own experience.

As to all suggestions and possibilities, we must always remain very open to what people suggest and to what life brings. We have to learn to respond continually to what comes to us in a living and true way. The rest will come by itself.

MARCH 18, 1956 I think that in order to help our children,

we have to reduce all we understand to its simplest terms, and then try to live by that. For children really are most deeply affected by example, and only secondly by explanation, when it is very simple and clear. Most important is that they should grow up in an atmosphere free from negativeness, and in which they are encouraged to be confident and to express their real selves. Teach them to be truthful, honest and sincere. That covers everything.

It seems very important that children should be encouraged to find their own beliefs and interpretations, not to imitate us—which they won't do in any case. It is important because it is on them that fulfilment of today's work depends.

CONSCIENCE

AUGUST 21, 1948 What a wonderful instrument for understanding is the idea of six activities*. This is a really esoteric idea, and seems the only one subtle and strong enough to be used in judging the development of esoteric work. Many people try to force everything into the division of good and evil. This is *not* an esoteric idea, but ordinary morality. And though it is good for ordinary life, it seems to lead to misunderstanding in our work. Because it means that many things are classed as evil which are not truly *criminal*, but only natural *growth* or natural *destruction*; while others must be classed as good which do not belong to *regeneration* (the only real good from our point of view) but perhaps to *healing* or *refinement*.

I feel it is of the greatest importance to learn to distinguish these six activities, and to understand that there are four which are 'natural' and we should try to observe with understanding; one which is always wrong and should always be rigidly excluded from all our surroundings; and a sixth which never happens by itself, but which we must struggle to introduce into everything we do. Even the attempt to understand this idea in itself introduces something of esotericism.

AUGUST 27, 1948 Many strange things may happen on the way of development: some paths that we once believed in turn out to be cul-de-sacs, while others we never paid much attention to disclose very extraordinary possibilities. At this stage there is only one guarantee of safety—and that is the gradual awakening of conscience. Without this, all other efforts are wasted, and esoteric work in the end can only turn to crime.

OCTOBER 17, 1948 Evidently at a certain point, in order to find one's way, it is absolutely essential to find conscience. No amount of guidance, no amount of obedience, can take its place. And strangely, guidance, taken in the wrong way, can even prevent conscience waking up. If he can touch or at least make it stir a little, conscience can show a man what is right and wrong for him in each particular emergency. It divides everything into right and wrong *for him*.

Without conscience, I am sure everything else, however promising, leads to a dead end. At the same time, when one gets away from one's own immediate duties and decisions, conscience is not enough. It cannot explain the larger world, nor even show how to understand it. A man who tries to apply his feeling of conscience, even supposing it is genuine, to the world, becomes what Ouspensky used to call a 'stupid saint'. For the larger world and all that goes on in it, cannot be judged on the basis of personal right and wrong. It is much too complicated for that.

Personally, I always wanted to 'understand' everything. But how can one 'understand' the extraordinary tangle of contradictory causes and tendencies with which we are surrounded in the world, sometimes well-meaning in intention, disastrous in result, useful in certain proportions, destructive in other proportions, and so on? How can one develop the right attitude to all this?

It seems to me more and more that the most extraordinary key to general understanding which was given us is the idea of six processes or six activities. The whole world is an immense complex of six different processes. Trying to force these into the simple conception of right and wrong—which is quite correct personally—produces every kind of distorted view and misunderstanding.

The idea of six processes is a very special idea—it seems to me really esoteric. If one studies everything from this point of view, I think gradually one's attitudes do begin to change. For example, as one begins to get the taste of the process called crime, one feels an urgent necessity to keep absolutely clear of its manifestations—not to have anything to do with them, not to admit them into one's surroundings, not to allow oneself to be interested in them. Interest in crime and destruction is, I am sure, a 'wire' that draws these processes towards us. So that after a time, if some criminal or violent or destructively accidental manifestation crosses one's path, one has an immediate movement of revulsion. One feels: 'This should not happen to me! What have I been doing to attract it? Careful!'

Then there are next four 'natural' processes, so to speak, which are neither good nor bad in themselves from our point of view, and are only to be observed, recognised.

And finally, there is this sixth process—of regeneration, esotericism—which cannot happen by itself, and which is our great interest. I feel that just as one has to acquire an 'instinctive' recognition of crime and avoidance of it, so one has also to develop a sense of intense attraction and discrimination towards this process. To do so it seems necessary to learn to recognise and reject all its imitations. Part of real school* work is to be able to distinguish the true from the false.

If one can purify one's sense of the 'esoteric' process in all this, and at the same time intensify one's interest and aspiration towards it, then I am sure the possibility exists of attuning oneself to very large forces indeed, about which we can certainly know very little in our present state.

Perhaps all this makes conscience and the idea of becoming sensitive to different activities too distant. Work upon them seems to be different. But in the end probably they should merge into a single emotional understanding, which could provide the guidance we need.

NOVEMBER 25, 1948 *Powers* and *being* are absolutely different things, and can develop or not, quite independently of each other. By powers I mean all innate or acquired capacities, from being able to lift a 100-pound sack to being able to levitate at will—and even including consciousness up to a certain point. Being is more difficult to explain, but you know what it means. It is difference in being which decides whether a strong man works for others, makes others work for him, or is too lazy to work at all. Strength belongs to powers, 'goodness', 'humanity', 'selflessness' and so on to being. The whole idea of development of being must be connected with making conscience.

So from this point of view one can almost put consciousness on one side, as belonging to powers, and conscience on the other, as belonging to being. But this is not quite right—*for beyond a certain degree of intensity* consciousness must wake conscience. There are certain principles in the universe that one cannot become conscious of without being touched in conscience.

DECEMBER 22, 1948 In order to come to a choice, each person has to examine himself in the deepest way; and this necessity is the best thing that can happen to one even though one may not feel ready to meet it. In some way we have to find *conscience* in ourselves; if we can find it this will tell us what our own attitude must be. Nothing else—no obedience, imitation, logic, fear—is going to help. Whatever we do to other questions, somehow we *have* to shake conscience awake. There is no guide but our conscience, or nearest to it, our deepest inner convictions. Conscience is the one thing we must find, and it will never fail us.

MAY 26, 1949 The brief flash of conscience tells us *in advance* exactly what the effects of different courses are going to be. As long as it works, only one course is possible—the other usually becomes impossible until conscience is put to sleep again. This is why, when for a second one knows what is necessary, it seems intensely important to do it right away, before conscience falls asleep again and other arguments supervene. For every time conscience is obeyed it seems to return more easily, while every time it is ignored it becomes less sensitive and more difficult to awake.

Probably all this should not really be called conscience. For if it were, it would be unbearable. But it is the intimation of conscience, the hint of conscience, so to speak.

The motion of the heart is so quick, so elusive—this is the trouble. So that, except with a constant listening, the motion of the mind always pours over it and swamps it.

It was said that conscience is 'an emotional understanding of the truth about oneself *in one particular instance*'. Everything lies in *this present* prompting. This is why all general ideas about conscience are so dangerous—they can easily help to keep it more asleep than ever.

AUGUST 15, 1952 It is clear that planetary influences have very different effects on different kinds of people. An influence that is inimical for a purely mechanical man may bring exceptional opportunity to the man who is following the way of conscience. There can be no general interpretations.

NOVEMBER 2, 1955 As conscience grows, self-importance dies.

NOVEMBER 20, 1955 All the gamut of reactions to higher Voices is in the story of Joan of Arc, and it does not seem to have changed at all since the fifteenth century. At the same time when one looks deeply into the period, that strange threshold from the Middle Ages into the Renaissance, one begins to feel that Joan was the instrument for presenting something very extraordinary indeed—the idea that an individual human being, having complete faith in her own conscience, in higher direction, in God, could be used to redeem a situation which had gone radically wrong. Somebody had to show that individual conscience is higher than all temporal authority, before the Renaissance could begin. She did it.

FEBRUARY 3, 1956 We must find our inner judgement, conscience if you like. There is no substitute for that. Sometimes fate pushes us into very tight corners to force us to find it for ourselves. When we begin to act from it, the results may look very odd indeed from outside; but they are *our own* actions, we reap the suffering and the profit, and by digesting that, *we* become strong and serviceable. There is no way of not making mistakes, and learning more from them than one ever could by being always right. I find it happens so often nowadays that one is faced with two possibilities—one day all laws, principles and profit seem to point to the first line as right, the other as disastrous, the next day things are so arranged to show one exactly the reverse. Then one is really left to one's own judgement. But it seems a more chastened judgement, in which either course may be made right and either wrong.

APRIL 12, 1956 Ask yourself sincerely: What do I want? Try to answer without self-criticism or sentiment. Learn to have confidence in the indications of conscience. When you have found in yourself a place of strength and security, guard it and establish yourself there.

MANHOOD AND WOMANHOOD

APRIL 30, 1949 It may sometimes be a bad fate to be a lady—but to be a woman, never! The only question is, what does it mean to be a woman? Evidently something very interesting indeed. But it means digging down very deep—giving up bad imitations of men's ideas, men's feelings and men's behaviour. To be a woman is something very positive. And I can understand that 'to become a woman' might be quite a big aim, just as 'to become a man' can be. Any negative attitude towards one's sex is an obstacle to development, while a positive attitude towards it may bring quite unexpected and extraordinary things.

AUGUST 20, 1952 Assisi is certainly alive with St. Francis—and St. Clare. They seem to have acted as a pair—like St. John of the Cross and St. Teresa. Evidently the really complete things have to be created by male and female together.

JANUARY 18, 1954 In the fourth way*, respect for sex and a positive attitude towards it are fundamentally necessary. Ouspensky insisted that nothing negative, either in thought or emotion, should be allowed to touch it; that all higher development began with sexual *normality*.

OCTOBER 2, 1955 Gurdjieff used to say: 'The trouble with the world is that men are not men and women are not women. Women have to learn to be women and men have to learn to be men.' Women have such a tremendous part to play, and to play it rightly they have to become free and sure of themselves. Of course, I do not mean free in any political or social sense. I mean they have to learn to be truly sincere and confident in the deepest part of themselves. Their work is always to bring men back to what is most true and simple and real. But in order to do so, they have to find this very very deep in themselves. They have to free men from all pretences and vanities and artificialities which go with their role of building and developing. But that means they have to find the living spirit within themselves.

JANUARY 11, 1956 Sexual desire is not the only form of love. It is tremendously important, and may carry deep spiritual love on its tide. But when it diminishes, the other forms of love must not be thrown away with it. They go still deeper into fate in the long run.

Sexual desire is not directly under our control. Though we can spoil it by thinking too much, worrying too much, by being ashamed or fearful. Curiously enough, the love of the soul and spirit is much more under our control. We have only to try to feel through our hearts without being too preoccupied with physical results.

People do not understand how deep the marriage relationship penetrates into one's fate. Marriage changes and grows and widens. Some things are left behind and others found. It grows through the man becoming more manly and the woman more womanly. People should think what it means to be a man and woman, what true relation of the sexes is, helping and completing each other.

To become more of a man means to be more responsible, more protective, more strong in every way, free of self-doubt and self-pity. The more a man can become a real man, the more will he help his wife to become a real woman. All of us are trying to become *real* men and *real* women. That is a very great and wonderful thing.

KNOWLEDGE

DECEMBER 19, 1946 For myself the idea of trying to remember, reconstruct and connect together all the different ideas of our system* has seemed very important. I notice in myself and in others such a tendency to stress one idea or one side, and work it to death, forgetting the many other explanations that must be connected, and other sides and obstacles which must be taken into account. And I feel that this is exactly how esoteric knowledge degenerates into ordinary religious or philosophical knowledge—esoteric knowledge is knowledge of the whole, ordinary knowledge is single ideas about a part taken separately.

AUGUST 29, 1948 Enormous amounts of detailed information on every conceivable branch of knowledge are available, and being constantly added to by the deductive method. But all this only leads to more confusion and division because such knowledge is not united by any principles. It is clear that only principles can reunite the different branches of knowledge and different sides of life which have become so separated and antagonistic.

It is true that any presentation of principles will not be accepted by ordinary scientists and scholars—but only those who have already guessed the existence of certain universal laws* and have begun to search for them. To others, these ideas will remain invisible.

Certainly new expressions of principles will be misinterpreted, just as religious, alchemical, magical, and other expressions were. 'Misuse' of principles is another thing, and is only possible, I believe, after an individual has had some considerable training and preparation. Ordinary readers cannot either use or misuse ideas—they can only be influenced by them or fail to see them.

SEPTEMBER 5, 1948 In principle I am convinced that our knowledge is a whole, and that nothing can be omitted for long, without its losing its special power. Omission often begins because people do not see the connection of some strange item of knowledge, and think Ouspensky put it in by whim or for amusement. Or else they think some subject 'too difficult for us'. So more and more things are left out, and in the end one is back at 'ordinary knowledge', 'ordinary morality'.

December 5, 1949 The visible universe is the only illustration of principles we have. Try to make a complete model of the enneagram*; you would have to go on till you had made a man or a world. Because the only complete expression of our system is a cosmos*; any less complete expression is a distortion of it.

It is a property of our logical mind to try to divide 'facts' and 'ideas' into two separate categories, calling 'facts' real, and 'ideas' unreal. As long as we do this I don't think we can come near the truth about things. For in the realm we are trying to penetrate 'facts' and 'ideas' are inseparable, 'facts' being as it were 'reflections' from 'ideas'. If one is more real than the other, it is the 'ideas' that are real and the 'facts' unreal.

April 18, 1951 I think the gap between principles and 'facts' —which disturbs many people—can be reduced, though probably it can never be eliminated altogether, by the very nature of the thing. For principles exist in a higher world, 'facts' in this one. When we focus on 'facts' we focus on this world, when we focus on principles we focus on another—and if we could really make them meet we should already have created the bridge between the two which is the whole Work.

November 12, 1951 Someone was telling me about his visit before the Finnish war to the monastery of Valamo, and of his attending there the very rare service of 'burial' over a monk who passes on to some exceptionally high degree. In his sermon about the meaning of this 'burial', the abbot said it might very well be the last time in history that such a service was performed, since only there and at Mount Athos was the tradition still understood.

As he described it, I felt that all esoteric forms—however beautiful—have their lifetime and their eventual death. And that it is not really wars and revolutions that destroy them, but simply that their time has come to an end. I suppose Valamo and Mount Athos have had nearly a thousand years. Probably that is a life on their scale. Only, it seems to me that before such ways die they have to make a memorial of their achievement in a form in which it can be transmitted forward into the new time, and later reabsorbed into the new esoteric work which shall grow in future.

NOVEMBER 15, 1951 I agree very strongly that a genuine unification has to be made between modern scientific knowledge (more and more amazing the more one studies it) and school* knowledge. This can and must lead within a generation or two to a real scientific mysticism or mystical science, which will I believe provide the real 'way' or 'form' of the age to come.

And all that can be done in this way displays more and more the magnificence of 'Tertium Organum' and 'A New Model', which tower higher and higher above all that comes after.

FEBRUARY 27, 1952 'Facts' are not what they are taken to be. The truth, the world, the body of man is so marvellous, subtle and intricate that no one can see the whole design. But each one who studies sincerely sees in this maze one particular pattern, each rather different from the next, yet right in its own way. If he works with understanding he may even build a whole 'system' upon his pattern, as the next student may on his. But what is wrong and leads to every kind of lying and distortion, is to try to force the two patterns to coincide, *outside of the knowledge of the whole.* We were always warned against comparing ideas in our system with ideas in other systems. This is logical mind at its most dangerous. For of course since the whole thing is put together from a different point of view, ideas never do coincide, and violence, lying and eventually the Inquisition have to be brought in to try to force them to do so. I wish I could express the freedom, joy and richness that comes from a deep feeling of diversity in unity, of the true 'harmony of the planets'. My planet can't sing the song of yours, nor yours of mine. But if several learn to sing *their own* we may hope that a harmony will result. I believe it will.

APRIL 2, 1952 The disadvantage of studying these ideas by oneself is that one becomes accustomed to taking the point of view of one type, one's own, as the only expression of esotericism. In a well-selected group it is exactly the variety of types and the necessity of including and reconciling all their particular points of view that opens the way to new horizons. Little by little one learns that in esotericism apparent contradictions are not of necessity mutually exclusive.

FEBRUARY 16, 1955 There is a tremendous and continual work to be done, relating the constant flow of new knowledge to the key principles we have been given. In the light of them, apparently insignificant discoveries and observations may sometimes start a completely new line of understanding.

It is clear that invisible School is making itself felt in our world in more and more different ways. It seems as though when men do the best they can in their own field, using their best techniques, their best invention and understanding, with least thought for themselves, at the peak of their achievement something quite incommensurable may be added momentarily from above. One recognises in scientific research, in books, and very much lately, it seems to me, in pictures [films] this unexpected element.

The direction of Higher School is very close to us. But it can be received consciously or unconsciously. We have been prepared to receive it consciously and with understanding. That is why a special key was given, so that some people should understand what was being done. But it does not mean that the same influence isn't being received in many other ways as well.

FEBRUARY 23, 1955 All human knowledge and experience must be looked at from the same point of view, that is, in relation to consciousness, cosmic laws, and man's approach to perfection. All knowledge is then seen to form one single whole.

JULY 20, 1955 We must try to watch where circumstances and opportunities lead us. We must learn as much as we can in every way, whether we can put it to immediate use or not. We all need much more knowledge, much more education to do what we have to do. Nothing that we learn is wasted.

AUGUST 13, 1955 Those who have been able to assimilate all the teaching into one coherent mental picture are very lucky—for whole it is, and in that lies its miraculous power.

To make this mental understanding live with our own experience and experiment is another thing. That may take a very long time. A whole lifetime or more. But it will come. At first we do not recognise the experience that life brings as having anything to do with the theory we know so well. Only afterwards we see the connection, and when we do, it enables us to digest the experience of life in quite a special way. It turns experience into understanding.

I listened to Ouspensky for eleven years, in lectures, with friends, and alone. At the end of that time, when at his death he actually performed the miracle* of change, I realised that no single thing that he ever said was irrelevant, that every phrase, public or private, was designed to help us understand the great mysteries when they should come our way.

So we must not forget the 'knowledge'. Only struggle to *live*; to be sincere, truthful and honest; to remember ourselves and forget our self-importance; truly and simply *to be*. The rest will come in time.

Everyone needs companions. Whether he joins some formal group of those who knew Ouspensky or Gurdjieff or Nicoll is a different question. But the company of those who are struggling to travel by the same path, he does need. For these truths are too hard for a single man alone to crack. He has to find others with whom he can exchange experience and understanding, share experiments. Then if they can put together what they individually discover, they may create a sufficiently strong field of understanding to attract attention and help. So people must keep their eyes open for their fellows. They may find them in very unexpected places.

UNDERSTANDING

July 30, 1948 Evidently the yielding up of the capacity of understanding is a very much more serious sin on the way of development than it appears. And no amount of other efforts can neutralise it.

The reason is that understanding is very closely connected with conscience, and that one who gives up the struggle to understand and simply accepts, must at a certain point stifle his own conscience. And from this one can only recover with very great suffering.

Understanding gives power and confidence; absence of understanding creates suffering and weakness—even though the individual may struggle bitterly.

It is interesting in this connection that people say: 'Collin Smith is teaching, will teach, won't teach.' They don't understand that I am *learning* and this is the only way that I or anyone else can do so. I remember very clearly sitting with Ouspensky at Longchamps in New York sometime about 1943, I think, and asking why everything seemed to have come to a stop. He said: 'You forget one thing; many people forget it—to learn more, you have to teach.'

Since then I have seen how many people, who had got very far, began to understand less and less, *because they were unwilling to accept responsibility for passing on to others what they understood.* Understanding cannot remain static—it can only increase or diminish; and the safest way to increase one's understanding is to help others to understand.

Actually this applies on all levels—though of course it cannot be said until the distinction between understanding and opinion is clear, and until various illusions of self-importance are broken. But it is a general principle.

October 7, 1948 The more one understands, the more one is forced to try every method and every experiment that may help to narrow the great gap between one's being as one observes it and the possibilities that one begins to glimpse. If understanding of the whole pattern of things and one's place in it grows, then one has no choice but to struggle. What one sees forces one on. Ouspensky used to say that the key of this way was 'understanding', and that every effort made with understanding of its reason and possible effect was worth ten times as much as the same effort made without understanding. With understanding, time and persistence, many things become possible.

October 27, 1948 I think it is a principle that sooner or later each person must find *right expression* for what he has understood. Anything which has no outward expression at all must be very suspect—it will be awfully like imagination. Right expression is a sort of magic which enables one to make transient understandings really one's own, and which may reveal new connections that one never suspected before. At the same time right expression doesn't necessarily mean talking, though it may include talking, if intentional and for a definite reason. For example, Ouspensky *wrote* many things in his books that he would practically never agree to talk about. Evidently each individual has to find his own right expression, some safe way of adding his understanding to the general stock, as well as preserving it for himself.

Perhaps if one can find a perfect method of expression it is not necessary to say anything. I think of Ouspensky, who for years explained in greatest detail the whole theory of change to a higher level of man, then gradually explained less and less, and finally became silent and *performed* the miracle*. Performance is the perfect expression and transcends every other.

December 15, 1948 Such an extraordinary power of new knowledge, understanding and certainty was released by Ouspensky's last work—before he died and at his death—that those people who opened themselves to it can never see things in the old way again. Particularly that time and achievement opened up quite new ideas both of the possibility of the Work and the purpose of it. In my own case, I feel that all my previous ideas were inexpressibly personal, trivial and lacking in daring, compared with what was finally made clear by Ouspensky.

We used to think it was our hope that was imagination; we were quite wrong—it is our doubts and fears which are imaginary and unnecessary, and prevent us from understanding anything. Energy comes from above, not below—everything is in that.

APRIL 3, 1949 How to keep an original line developing with emotion and without deviation? The only practical answer I have found is 'people'. The pressure of people from many different sides—if one really exposes oneself to their questions, requirements, hopes, demands—can provide the force to drive one forward, provided one holds the rudder straight.

I remember once in a very bad time indeed sitting with Ouspensky at Longchamps and asking why everything seemed to have come to a dead stop. He said: 'You forget that in order to learn, you have to teach.' I wouldn't put it like that now. But I do see that if the pressure of others—some who require you to be better than you know, others who tempt you to be as weak as you were, those who ask questions whose answers you can only learn in trying to answer, those whom you have to force yourself to ask, the man who can talk about recurrence, and the deformed beggar who catches your leg as you walk along the street, the man above and the man below—all these push you if you don't spare yourself, and it is up to you to *make them push you in the right direction.* Their pressure never relaxes, it is only we who have schooled ourselves not to notice it.

The only other thing which I have found to produce the same effect is the pressure of ideas requiring to be expressed—in writing, painting or something like that. And curiously enough this is pressure of people—those from whom the ideas come and those to whom they must go. But at second hand, so to speak.

MAY 24, 1949 If one man really achieves higher states in which he experiences different parts of the universe, and different states of time and matter, he may—in favourable circumstances—be able to convey this to those in sympathy with him as understanding.

But such a state as Ouspensky reached was evidently outside time* as we experience it, so that what was real then is equally real now, and just as able to produce this kind of reflection in our minds today as it was in October 1947—*if we can bring ourselves to the receptive state to which he intentionally raised us.* For this, an intensely positive attitude towards Ouspensky, the sacrifice of all our personal doubts and sufferings, and great and prolonged attention are certainly necessary.

But *it is possible*—this is the chief thing.

Things like experiment with diet can give us a start. One must become as physically well as possible. What one sometimes feels as inertia is a purely physical state, and one has to deal with it by physical means: reasonable diet, exercise, drinking water, and so on.

Only nothing should be exaggerated—and any experiments should be for a definite and limited period. Later one can repeat them or try other experiments. It is not good to let any discipline become too fixed. Ouspensky said: 'Learn to make demands upon yourself.' This is the secret. But it applies to all sides of oneself—physical, emotional, mental. And one kind of demand should never become such a habit that it makes one forget all the other kinds.

JULY 25, 1949 I am sure that everything which comes to us from a higher source must in turn be expressed by us, if we are to take advantage of it. In school*, influences must flow from above down and through one person and another and so, more diluted but equally necessary, out into life. Each person through whom this influence flows learns and benefits. But the one with whom the influence stops, gets nothing and can understand nothing. He is like the end of a blocked-off water pipe where no water moves.

All the same, I don't mean that there need be any formal expression. Some people may express and pass on influence in a very undefinable way, just by being. It is different for everybody.

JANUARY 22, 1952 Understanding more, seeing things more objectively, comes first; when that sinks in thoroughly enough, one begins to *be* different, act differently. There isn't any other way.

MARCH 13, 1952 As Ouspensky always said, this is the way of *understanding. Everything* must be understood, and being understood, everything from the popular to the esoteric, from the tango to Catholic prayers, can reveal interior connections.

JUNE 10, 1952 At those times when understanding suddenly widens, day by day more and more, one should leave traces of how the crack that lets in the light of new understanding was opened. These traces have a very special flavour and strength, and one day in their turn will produce effects. They also help to fix the new understanding. For when suddenly without warning we find ourselves in the middle of that which we have been seeking, we should remember the necessity of fixing the state that has been given us, in order for it to become permanently ours.

These times of sudden enlightenment and understanding are part of the most mysterious and miraculous aspect of the Work. We cannot anticipate them, we cannot deserve them. 'We do not know the day nor the hour . . .' as it is said in the Gospels. But when they come, all values are upset. And they fix the direction and the course of the whole of the stage that follows.

JULY 1, 1952 In a highly emotional state we are flooded by emotions and visions. The wave of emotion will inevitably subside. But the task is to fix the understanding that it brings in order that this understanding may remain even when the emotion that brought it has gone. To *fix* a new attitude—towards oneself, towards other people, towards one's teacher and towards God—this is the problem. The person in whom new attitudes are fixed, permanent, reliable, can be the instrument of higher powers.

JULY 8, 1952 I am glad when people tell me their experiences and new understandings. But we must also be prepared for the lean days. We must store uncompleted understandings in order to digest them and nourish ourselves with them in those times when further 'supersubstantial bread' is not given. There is so much to do—we must work for the bad times as well as for the good.

SEPTEMBER 9, 1952 An individual life may be quite rich, good and satisfactory, without the power of organisation. In the ordinary way, it is made up for by other qualities. But in our way, one has to be able to 'organise' to the full all that passes through one's hands and one's understanding—we must have organised thoughts, organised effort, organised knowledge. It is part of the economy of esotericism—question of the 'talents'.

SEPTEMBER 12, 1952 Sometimes one finds in people real and deep perception mixed with personal prejudices and wild shots in the dark. How Ouspensky used to struggle with us about 'lying', that is, speaking of what one does not know as though one knew. One did not understand properly then, now it becomes clearer. It is not so serious in a state of ignorance; it is when one *does* begin to learn and know something that lying becomes so dangerous. For it prevents the proper use of that which one does know.

FEBRUARY 13, 1953 I've come to the conclusion that if we can't express a thing in the simplest possible terms, we haven't really understood it.

OCTOBER 22, 1953 I think the deep instinct to check everything, verify everything, seems absolutely essential. In fact it is this friction between the instinct to believe and the instinct to question which forces us to that state of self-remembering* where alone things can be truly assessed.

NOVEMBER 9, 1953 We cannot communicate understanding 'raw'; first we must purify it, then skim off the personal dross, and finally mint it into a form acceptable by others.

The beauty of a nice shocking series of questions is that everybody *has* to answer these questions for himself. Nobody else's answer is valid for him. A kind of half-belief, within strictly reasonable limits, is altogether too comfortable.

When the verification comes to what we believe, it always seems like a little miracle. And we *have* to demand verification for what we believe. Only, my verification and my little miracles don't mean a thing to anyone else, and they're not supposed to. This is sometimes difficult to accept. But it is arranged like that. If little miracles were valid for third parties, the Work would be drowned in a flood of superstition.

MAY 11, 1954 Things grow and unfold as they must. But each individual's opportunity seems to lie in how much he can see and understand the general growth as it takes place: the more he understands this process of big growth the more useful he will be.

DECEMBER 10, 1954 We were taught—and I understand it better every day—that understanding is not the product of one function* in man, but the resultant of several functions working in harmony. For example, if one appreciates something with the mind, one 'knows' it; if one appreciates it with the emotions, one 'feels' it; if one appreciates it with the external physical organs, one 'senses' it. But if one simultaneously appreciates it with the mind, emotions and physical senses, then one really *understands* it. This is very rare as we are. It can be developed. But in order to do so, something like 'self-remembering' is necessary—that is, one has to remember *all* one's functions and their relations to the thing in question.

Modern mathematics is a powerful tool of thought, not only in the physical sciences, but also in relation to life itself. Only, for this, one has to understand mathematics not only with the mind, but also with the emotions and the whole physical organism. 'Emotional mathematics' can solve any problem in the universe. After all, what else is the idea of the Holy Trinity?

FEBRUARY 12, 1955 I feel very vividly the knitting up of new understanding which is going on all over the world. For it is going on, far faster and far deeper than any of us dream, I believe. It really is the key of a new harmony which has to reconcile all things hitherto unreconcilable.

August 14, 1955 What relationships are living in the Work continue to develop and grow, whether near or far. We must not try to force understanding between group and group, but leave it to develop naturally between the individuals who are in sympathetic contact. It is, after all, the growth of individual souls that we are really interested in.

August 25, 1955 By understanding everything becomes simple. We see what is, objectively. Where we stand, objectively. What we can do, objectively. Understanding avoids useless friction, pointless struggle. Makes us steady, tolerant, kind, 'understanding'. Gives us weight. To reach real understanding we must study more, much more, verify in worldly terms all that has been said or felt.

Being open. Everything is available, waiting for us. We are bathed in cosmic radiations, all help. But we have to make ourselves open. Open our pores. Catch everything. What prevents us from being open, receiving what is going, is being preoccupied with ourselves, thinking of ourselves. If we forget ourselves, everything comes to us.

Polarities. Sun—Earth. North Pole—South Pole. Positive terminal—Negative terminal. Man—Woman. Everything real is created by the intervention of an invisible force in the field of tension between two poles. The two poles are reconciled by some higher current, something unrecognised. Then creation begins. If the third element is not present or not recognised, the polarity may turn to hostility, violence, destruction, hatred. The poles seem 'enemies'. Where the third force* is invoked, they are complements. Seeing the reconciliation of polarities by third force is the beginning of harmony. Ouspensky once said, long ago: 'There are ideas which could stop all quarrels; such an idea is the law of three.'*

IMAGINATION

JANUARY 11, 1950 Remember that there are two kinds of imagination: to imagine what is false to be true, but also, to imagine what is true to be false. One may be shown the way out from the first; but how can one be shown the way out from the second?

JUNE 6, 1952 I know what people mean when they say that life becomes more like poetry every day. I think it should be like this, and to a much more intense degree than anything we know now. Poetry is free movement, a kind of magic of the celestial rhythm. Our trouble is that we are still much too inert.

There is only one danger from the poetic feeling. That is that it turns inwards, and becomes imagination, separates us from other people. When it works as it should, it always connects us in a living way with all kinds of people and things, breaks down barriers, and makes us free of a bigger world.

DECEMBER 15, 1952 Ouspensky used to say that people were divided into three kinds, those whose chief difficulty was negative emotion, those whose chief difficulty was imagination, and those whose chief difficulty was formatory [mechanical] thinking.

FEBRUARY 15, 1952 The problem for all of us is how to distinguish between the help we receive and what our own imagination conjures up round it. It does not mean to say that we must have no imagination, nor that we must not elaborate things for ourselves. But we must know what is original and what we have added. Otherwise all becomes confused. Self-remembering* is the magic talisman in this process. In moments of self-remembering we know the answer, we know our place, we have no pretensions, only certainty.

DIFFERENT 'I's — REAL AND FALSE

JANUARY 18, 1950 I have been reading Psalms 139 and 140 again—how wonderful they are when taken as the cry of a man who knows his own 'I's*, how incomprehensible taken any other way.

'Search me, O God, and know my heart; try me, and know my thoughts . . .'—if a man can cry that continuously with all his force, he is on the right way. He doesn't have to worry about the rest.

NOVEMBER 14, 1951 One way it seems to me 'I's can be studied is this: There are 'I's which arise from each function* of essence* and from each imagination of personality*. For example, there may be 'I's connected with travel or physical activity, that have their root in moving function; other 'I's evoked by churches, old rituals, holy places might have their root in emotional function; others again not in essence at all, but in some dream or fear or longing.

If it be taken like this, then these essential 'I's at any rate could be taken as being the same material as the energy with which their parent function works.

JUNE 15, 1952 We have been speaking about the idea of hidden 'I', that original spark of divine energy which gives rise to a life, and will still be there untouched after it is over. We felt all ordinary uses of this word 'I' as a strange kind of forgetfulness, as if all the different organs and opinions borrowed the name because the original owner of the name had disappeared and been forgotten. And because the original idea of 'I' is connected with the deepest and truest instincts of self-preservation, all the voices which steal the word also steal the sense of importance attached to it and feel that everything to which it is applied must also be justified and supported at any cost. We felt that if it were possible to take the word away from all the voices which use it now and restore it to its true meaning, our whole attitude would change to something quite different. This line of thought seemed to touch something very deep.

AUGUST 25, 1952 One has to look quietly at all one's qualities and capacities, and see really what one has at one's disposal. I think it is not a question of condemning some and praising others, but of looking at them all as apart from one's real central 'I', as the tools which one's innermost self has available, so to speak. For example, if one is sensual, it is not one's sensuality, it is one's body's sensuality, and it wouldn't be a strong healthy body if it didn't have its own strong sensuality, through which one can learn a great deal about the world that couldn't be learned in any other way. If this sensuality gets loose, and starts acting on its own account, calling itself I, then it may get one into all kinds of trouble. But as an instrument, as a servant, as something at the disposal of the innermost self, it is a wonderful thing. And so with all one's other qualities.

SEPARATION OF THE REAL AND FALSE

JUNE 20, 1949 In *In Search of the Miraculous*, Ouspensky wrote that he came to the realisation that nothing right could ever be achieved by violent means. And I feel that this even applies to what is called 'work on oneself'. Just as the knots of personal relationships in life cannot be cut, but only untied, so I believe that the process of inner change is one of patiently, continuously loosening the bonds of fascination, and substituting an attachment, an interest, an inner sensitiveness to higher influences. Violence may sometimes give interesting material. I do not think it is a method of permanent building. The idea is very well expressed in the old Zen problem: 'There is a live chicken in a bottle—how do you get it out without either breaking the bottle or killing the chicken?' Nothing should be broken. And nearly always violence breaks things.

NOVEMBER 25, 1950 All that Ouspensky did and said at that time seemed to me to have exactly this purpose and effect—to sort out the people who could respond to the miraculous from those who could not, and also to sort out in those people themselves the small part which could respond from the large part which was unable to do so. It was very clear that if a man in a higher state of consciousness acts directly from the perceptions of that state, without bothering to consider the fashions and weaknesses of ordinary life, he will seem mad to men in an ordinary state. Evidently great teachers have to soften their truth to the understanding of their hearers, to be 'gentle' with them—but for a short time their work may exactly consist in not compromising with ordinary life at all. This will be the real test of those who have studied with them, and will show whether they have really understood or have heard only words. 'From that time many of his disciples went back, and walked no more with him.'

This same test is probably connected with the dying of the

old personality. Certainly there is plenty of room for this personality to adapt itself to lectures, philosophical discussion, ecclesiastical organisation, and so on. And evidently there comes a time when a real teacher has to create conditions which are unbearable for the old personality of those about him. He does this by acting, without compromise, from his higher understanding, without any concessions to the ways of the world. This is literally unbearable to what is artificial in his followers—either they must go away or something must die in them.

All work for development has two sides—something old in man has to be killed and something quite new has to be born. Preparation for the one and the other must go side by side, and they require quite different work. It can happen (though very rarely) that the old can be killed in a man without the new being born; then he is lost, at sea, at the mercy of every outside influence, open to 'seven devils worse than the first'. It can also happen that the new can be born without the old being killed; then all his new perceptions, understandings, powers will be flavoured with a personal outlook, will serve his chief weakness. The balance is very tricky. This is exactly why school is necessary at a certain point.

I do not think any man can kill off his own personality by himself. Only a man who knows far more than he can give it the final blow. But he can gradually starve it, gradually—after long self-observation—learn to know its characteristics and withdraw himself from them. Like a nut which ripens, his kernel can gradually shrink from the shell and become separate from it. Then only a light blow will break the shell and reveal the kernel. But if the nut is green, a blow that would break the shell would also crush the kernel. So the pupil must work, and the teacher must know.

DECEMBER 27, 1950 All a man's life, thoughts, feelings, hopes, surroundings, attachments, karma, which have hitherto developed in relation to this world, have to be intentionally 'reconstructed' *in relation to the world in which he wants to be born.* For example, a man has made hundreds of acquaintances, friends, enemies during his lifetime in relation to this present world and to the sympathies and antipathies of his physical body which belongs to it. Regeneration means that all these relationships have to be intentionally and individually reconstructed, each one placed on a completely new basis, under new laws. I don't think the extent of this reconstruction of one's life in relation to other people is fully seen yet. People still think very subjectively about the whole thing—'it will be better *for me* if I can eliminate negative emotions', and so on. They don't understand that this subjective element is exactly what makes reconstruction impossible. Because it is reconstruction of everything on the basis of laws, *instead* of subjective feelings.

If we try to serve something greater than ourselves, then it becomes clear that we have to reconstruct ourselves in order to be able to do so. If we try to reconstruct ourselves without this, then we base the reconstruction exactly on that which has to be left out. I see some people make big efforts, take their faults terribly seriously, make tremendous admissions about themselves, and only become more subjective than before. To me this does not belong to the activity which leads to escape. For that activity means reconstruction of everything, ***with the old self left out.*** Only this really leads to the possibility of rebirth in a higher world *as an innocent baby.*

Crime is the obverse of all this. It is that which becomes more subjective, more fixed, and leads others too into its narrower and narrower circle. It can never exist in the same scene as the activity of regeneration, just as the heads and tails of a penny can never be seen together, for if you begin to study the one the other must disappear. Yet both together make the penny, as both regeneration and crime make the upward and downward movement of the universe. In the universe as a whole, something must fall that another thing may rise. The laws represented by the devil take care of that: we must not have anything to do with it. Yet perhaps we have to make a sacrifice to the devil. Perhaps we have to leave our old selves behind to go to hell, while we ourselves go to heaven. If one remains subjective, one will be torn in two over that. But if one can cease to be subjective one will simply say 'good riddance'—and the great balance will be maintained.

SEPTEMBER 29, 1951 Each man lives in a prison which he has been building for himself all his life. The great thing is to cease restoring it. Certainly, even if he does learn something new, stops reinforcing the prison walls, and begins work on a different dwelling, the prison may still remain standing round him for some time till the new is ready and the old crumbles for lack of attention. But the fact is that the prison is perpetuated by the repetition of the weaknesses, indecisions, compromises which originally created it. If they are changed or turned, little by little the prison must melt away for lack of restoration.

We cannot alter the present; it is no use crying over the fact. But we can alter the future. First we have to believe that a way out exists for us. In fact it does, but it will do us no good until we believe in its existence and gradually transfer more and more of our attention to it.

We can try and see if there is one task in our business life, and one habit in our home life that we can do henceforward from the point of view of the future, and of what we want to become. This may create a crack through which other things can enter.

JANUARY 27, 1952 When people reach a certain stage of development, and there is one feature which they are not willing to give up, the devil can and does work through this feature. In all the rest of their being these people may be good, wise, understanding and very necessary to the Work—this is what makes it so difficult.

My question is, how to deal with it? I do not believe that rules are the answer, for this activity can use rules a good deal more cleverly than we can. I do not believe that it is a question of frightening people, because that tends to drive it into the dark where it is more elusive even than now. I believe that where possible, the answer lies in enlisting the understanding support of the other (true) side of the same person. We have to appeal to a level *beyond* that on which the devil manifests. Once in New York, Ouspensky said, speaking of the lateral octave of the ray of creation: 'Can you find at what point the devil enters?' I think that was the clue. Our target must be above that point. It's the only safe place.

MARCH 5, 1952 We once came to the idea that the devil worked on the planetary level but did not work on the solar level; that he could eat souls but not spirits.

If this is right, what can we do? Nothing, I believe, but appeal with all our force to a level above the devil, appeal directly to the world where the sun always shines and there are no shadows, because all things are themselves radiant there. This, I believe, is the great safeguard of those who in all ages believed in God and were able, even naively, to appeal directly to God. If they did so sincerely, and as long as they did so, they became free of danger.

MAY 14, 1952 I feel that much of that which people call evil is not evil at all, but really destruction. I mean it refers to that one of the six cosmic processes* which can be given this name. On the other hand I begin to have a more and more healthy respect for real evil—that is to say corruption, which belongs to that different degenerative cosmic process to which Ouspensky gave the name of crime. Particularly, this corruptive process becomes significant when it begins to touch the result of esoteric work. If people begin to change or acquire something, and this new 'something' is touched with poison—this to me is big evil, a kind of evil which I never guessed before. It seems to begin when one strong feature or habit or side of life is left out from the general work of consciousness. If the divorce is complete, then this abandoned feature may even acquire a kind of independent life of its own and become a tool of corruptive forces. Probably this was what Stevenson meant with Jekyll and Hyde.

I feel that one of the devil's best tricks is to persuade us to attach the word 'evil' to trivial things, thus leaving us with no convenient name by which to recognise his major works.

SEPTEMBER 24, 1952 Destroying false personality seems to be half the whole work. Something we have and don't need has to die, and something we have not but do need has to be born. All work is preparation for either one or the other of these two things.

I do not think one can 'destroy' false personality oneself, but gradually one can become more and more loose from it, less and less committed to it; so that one day when the right shock comes to us from outside, it will fall away of itself and we can emerge free. Meanwhile I think we have to learn to accept ourselves, as we have to learn to accept others. Accept our own clowning, trickiness, failures and go on to a new impartial viewpoint which lies beyond them. Difficult to describe. But no violence, even against oneself.

March 11, 1956 No one can invent 'pressure' of work. Pressure is produced by the conditions of life, by seeing life as it is. We all have our habits, physical and mental—like buffers—to lessen or soften the pressure of life. By freeing ourselves from these habits, pressure grows by itself—the pressure of responsibility, of commitments, of investigations to be done, aims to attain.

CONTRADICTIONS

JANUARY 3, 1953 When one realises the part fear plays in human life, one sees the true key to all misery and slavery. Each type* can live either dominated by fear or free from it. Each type has its own characteristic fears—the instinctive man fears illness, the ambitious man fears failure, the emotional man fears losing his relations and friends, etc. Studying the different kinds of fear is also a way of studying types—though not a very amusing way!

APRIL 2, 1953 Regarding free circulation as the condition of health—it is very clear that strong circulation brings health and new possibilities to all parts of an organism. Where there is constriction, disease strikes. I think that is true on all scales. It is obviously so in the body. But also in one's lifetime, where memory is that which circulates. Those parts or incidents in our lives, which we do not want to remember, begin to fester, and their poison may spread even into the present in all kinds of fears and prejudices. On the other hand, by full memory of the past, what we now understand and hope for can flow back into it, cure it, change its nature.

One sees just the same in a group. When ideas and feelings flow freely and with confidence among all the people in it, there is health and life. Where an obstacle grows, and someone misunderstands another and won't listen to them, again poisons develop, so the prejudice has to be melted out or the quarrel put right, before circulation and the group can be made well again.

When we remember wrong things we did, a kind of inflammation develops. There is a clash between what we actually did and what we have since come to feel to be right. Our present ideas, carried on the stream of memory, like white corpuscles in the blood, meet a poisoned place and try to heal it. Until they do so, the place may be very painful and inflamed. It is a sign that something is happening.

OCTOBER 22, 1953 While some people are enslaved by blaming

others, some are equally enslaved by blaming themselves. It is the same thing. Freedom is when one sees oneself impartially as one does an interesting stranger, without praise or blame.

SEPTEMBER 3, 1954 Life is very hard on those who see contradictions in others, but not in themselves.

ACCEPTANCE

DECEMBER 16, 1948 How to go against fate? I can only recommend you to the Book of Job. For evidently we cannot go against fate. Fate depends on the past and there is nothing we can do about it. The secret, I think, is that we can pass *through* our fate in quite different ways. Usually people let the fate created by this past arouse in them, and thus in others, reactions which will certainly create exactly similar fate in the future—just as one echo produces another. This is what is unnecessary. Somehow, we have to accept what fate brings, not rebel against it, but swallow it and make of it something advantageous to oneself.

In the last years with Ouspensky, one of the most extraordinary things was to see how he turned every unfavourable trick of fate—separation from his friends, distortion of his ideas, physical weakness and pain—into advantages, and by willingly abandoning normal powers and faculties was enabled to achieve supernormal ones of infinitely greater value. It was as though every time the normal reaction would have been to make some demand of the outside world, he instead made an equivalent or greater demand upon himself. In this way he became free.

FEBRUARY 1, 1949 There is something very interesting about the law of cause and effect. It seems clear that all the causes we have created in our lives and whose effects we have not experienced, must be lying dormant until the unexpected day when—taken by surprise, we call the inevitable result accident. Sooner or later all 'unfinished business' must be finished, and all books balanced. The wise man tries to pay off his debts *before* the bills are presented; tries to settle the loose ends of his life, at any rate in his mind, if he cannot in actuality. And every payment required of him in life, he meets eagerly, glad to pay off another instalment. Somehow this understanding seems to produce the desire to *accept* everything that comes, not to struggle against it. As Ouspensky accepted, even intensified, illness, old age, pain, loneliness. One becomes free by swallowing—a deep breath, a gulp, and down it all goes.

Then along with the question of becoming free of one's own chain of cause and effect, comes the other question of how to become attached to cause and effect of a different nature. This seems connected with the possibility of accepting as one's own the effects of causes set up by one's teacher. In the course of all those years, Ouspensky threw out countless suggestions as to different lines of work and experiment; by picking them up now one becomes part of the causes and effects of his life. He or his books touched innumerable people and awakened a certain curiosity, which by force of circumstances could never be directly satisfied by him. By cherishing this curiosity in the people we come across and feeding it as best we can, we again become in some way connected with *his* chain of cause and effect, which little by little can tend to supersede our own.

What does it mean, to become free? Free of what? Free for what? And how is it done? This is the question.

In that last time, Ouspensky seemed to show so clearly how. By accepting everything that life and death could bring, by not resisting, he became free.

We struggle and turn and twist because we do not see the future. If you do see the future, as he evidently saw it, you accept it—there is nothing else to do. And in accepting, you yourself become free. Now I begin to see the significance of wanting to know the future. The man who knows the future does not kill himself trying to alter what must be. He accepts what must be, swallows it, and in this way rises above it. *Then* everything becomes possible for him.

FEBRUARY 7, 1949 All circumstances—good or bad—must change in time; and if one can only pass through them equally, without being borne too much up or too much down, one becomes ready for other change. It is not the happy or tragic role that makes the difference between actors, but the way the role is played. Some parts of life are very hard. At the same time one can no longer wish it to be otherwise; for perhaps it is better to be called upon to pay up to the limit of one's capacity for a while, so that one's debt to life is reduced, and one may be that much nearer to becoming free.

Though we do not know how it works, I am very sure that this paying off of accumulated debts is essential before really new things can enter one's life, from a different level.

NOVEMBER 24, 1950 If one can learn to accept Fate, gradually acceptance makes one free. It is very unwise to try to bully Fate—one can only bully something one's own size.

JUNE 3, 1952 I believe that in writing one must not think about immediate results at all. One must just go on writing what one has to as well as one possibly can. And when it is finished, go on to something that will be better still. After some time it seems as though there is a great accumulation of written pages that nobody is ever going to read. But books and writings have their own individual time of gestation, and one day when one is least expecting it and has really become quite impartial towards them, they do decide to get themselves published. They get born when they are ready, and not before.

AUGUST 15, 1952 How can we learn to accept fate, which is only bringing us that which we must meet in any case? I do not think it means bearing hardly on oneself. For over and over again, one sees that those who are hard on themselves are equally hard on others, while those who are easy on others are easy on themselves. This is a question of type, not of change. The way out does not lie there.

I think one must learn acceptance in another new and deeper sense, as Ouspensky practised it in those last months. All the contradictions in people—can one not accept them, swallow them? The earth does; God does; men are not struck by lightning for contradicting themselves—at any rate not for the first million times or so. And how shall we accept the great tests which fate brings us if we cannot accept the annoying inconsistencies of our friends?

When a person is accepted into a group, he is accepted with all he is, all he is going to be. The group calculates the total risk and takes it. It cannot say, 'We'll have this feature but not that; we'll have his head but not his legs.' It takes him as he is, and becomes responsible for all his mistakes in return for sharing in all his achievements. And each person who enters a group tacitly makes this bargain in relation to all the others.

But I think we have not only to learn to accept others in this way, we have also to accept ourselves—with all our history, our habits, tendencies and hopes and sins, past present and future. Only when the whole is *fully accepted*, does the slow work of healing and reconstruction begin. As long as we are trying to perform impossible amputations on ourselves or on others, no true healing can begin, because *acceptance* is not yet understood.

Sometimes it seems to me that the pill which the sly man swallowed, and gained at once what the others worked for, for years, was 'things as they are, myself as I am'.

Perhaps there is still something missing. How can one accept fate if it has no meaning? I can only say that this idea became alive for me when I began to see fate as Providence—the inevitable result of one's past which, swallowed, can make one free of that past. The working of God in individual life. That is an immense relief.

JULY 1, 1953 First, most of us feel rather pleased with ourselves and proud of our endeavours. Then after quite a long time that begins to wear thin and one grows ashamed and unhappy about oneself. It is a painful period. Later one begins to cotton on to a secret. One learns to swallow oneself, gifts, weaknesses and all, without either inner praise or blame. One begins to see oneself as just a poor devil like all the other human beings round one. They are not to be blamed, nor the instrument one has to work with oneself. They must be treated reasonably and tolerantly, so must one's own machine. After that things begin to change, but not in the way one expected.

FEBRUARY 3, 1955 It is very lucky to be an optimist. Though whether one is lucky because one is an optimist, or an optimist because one is lucky, I still don't know. In any case I am both in a superlative degree.

ACCEPTANCE

March 8, 1955 The first thing that helps us to remove old attitudes is to accept oneself. Self-remembering* means acceptance—of oneself, of others, of all that is. In the past we have all been so preoccupied with our own problems that there was neither time nor interest to give to real things. Now we have to accept ourselves as we are, and understand that all *that* doesn't really merit much attention. Then one is free to devote oneself to something really interesting—the Great Work. This is true freedom. We must try to forget ourselves in the big vision of what has to be done.

November 15, 1955 It is very difficult for people who are whipping their own top faster and faster to realise that it is themselves who make it spin and nobody else.

POSITIVE ATTITUDE

OCTOBER 11, 1948 There is a state—like that of a small child or a shipwrecked man washed up naked on an island—when everything that exists must be accepted. All that you are is your body and the life-force which motivates it. So there is nothing with which you can feel negative emotions. In trying to answer the question: 'Who am I?', one may come to certain answers which produce almost the same effect.

From such states one knows that condemnation and negative criticism are always and everywhere wrong. They lead nowhere and can only spoil everything. When one has this understanding about negative emotions one is in one way very safe, and in another way very vulnerable. It is natural to believe the best of everything, and I think it is important to remember that there are also harsh laws connected with development—at least they may appear harsh through limited understanding.

APRIL 30, 1949 At one very emotional moment in those last days, Ouspensky said: 'People must not be afraid to take second step.' It seemed and still seems to have two sides. First of all, it seems connected with a quite new scale of attention, *permanent* attention, remembering *all the time*, as a continual state. We have to demand from ourselves. But it also seemed connected with the realisation that quite new things *are possible*, that higher influences are much nearer than we thought, and that with their help our ordinary self, the machine, can *actually* be transcended. These two sides are inseparable, each impossible alone, but each making the other possible.

Only one has to believe that it is possible. The slightest breath of doubt, not only of those higher forces but of oneself, immediately seems to cut one off from new possibilities. Perhaps one has not only to believe new things possible, but to be sure that they will come.

Perhaps all this is connected with third force* in the work of change. We may see and actually bring together first and second force, effort and mechanicalness. But it is third force which is so elusive, which can't be compelled or cajoled or even calculated, but if all is favourable, may suddenly and inexplicably descend. It once came to me that *this* can never be deserved. It must always be regarded as a gift.

Early one morning, shortly before his death, Ouspensky suddenly said: 'One must do everything one can—and then just cry to . . .' He did not finish, just made one big gesture upwards.

Unremitting efforts, the gradual development of will—this is creation of right active force. But always there is third force, unknown, incalculable. Is it reverence, is it faith, is it certainty, is it knowledge, is it love? I don't know. Perhaps all and more. But it can't be left out; and somehow it can make everything possible—even against reason.

June 18, 1949 There is a level at which the devil *cannot* enter. The whole idea must be to get there. If we cannot, we must at least remember that such a level does exist. Crime cannot exist in the face of positive emotion. If we cannot have positive emotion, we can still remember that it is the one, the only safeguard in the long run.

May 1, 1950 I think faith is the same as that which Ouspensky called 'positive attitude'. And in my experience I know that was the first essential, whose presence made the impossible possible, and whose absence immediately cut one off from all understanding. During the last months and weeks of his life, when all was so strange, new, unreasonable, faith that what was being done had meaning, had purpose, immediately seemed to open the door to understanding of that purpose, however deep and unknown. While if for a moment that faith was lost, what was being done actually became for the doubter no more than the vagaries of an old man who had lost his mind. And so remained till faith returned. So certainly my experience is that what the Roman Catholic Church says about faith was at that time and since not a whit too strong.

December 24, 1950 Some people have faith and others positive scepticism. By faith I mean a kind of knowing beyond one's powers. By positive scepticism I mean an intense questioning of everything until the truth is reached that way. Maybe it will be a long while before the two paths meet. But honestly followed they must meet in the end. And it seems to me to be as useless for one who has not faith to pretend to have it, as for one who has it to pretend he has not. Only if it does begin to dawn, and one begins to know things one could not know, then it is very important not to be afraid of it, or argue oneself out of it, or allow oneself to be argued out of it.

MARCH 18, 1951 If one can get near enough to the source, it is impossible to be negative. But even as I write that, I think—what a hopelessly negative way of expressing it! And how little this describes the positive understanding, the positive certainty, the positive love which fills the place left by the departure of negativeness! And what immense vistas begin to open up!

School*, for instance. Once upon a time school meant a wise man teaching foolish men. Now one sees school behind school behind school. Big school seems now like the highest function of the earth; the mechanism of consciousness not only for mankind but for the planet. The rise and fall of civilisations are only the play of big school. And behind big school on earth, there is the greater school of the Solar System; and even —I am sure—connection with a still higher directing force on a certain star.

NOVEMBER 14, 1951 What is very difficult for people to understand about the case of a child with a handicap from birth is that it implies *absolutely nothing wrong* in the fate of either parents or the child. Without formulating it to themselves, people believe that it must mean there was a mistake, a wrong action, a 'sin' somewhere. On the contrary, often such children and their parents are much freer of negativeness than most families. To me, it seems that there are souls who, for certain reasons of growth, are required to pass through these very difficult forcing conditions of control and consciousness, and that families are chosen for them previously where there will be much more love, affection and understanding available than ordinarily. The love and belief of the parents and certainty in their children provides exactly the third force which can enable their 'inner selves' to use this special state of their bodies to achieve what is thus made possible for them to achieve.

AUGUST 20, 1952 One sees how a man who gives up *everything*—like St. Francis—has unlimited power. Nothing is impossible. Talk about positive attitude! When everyone else in Christendom was talking of the Crusades, he said: 'Why, it's quite simple—we'll convert the Sultan.' And he went and tried.

He lay down on the bare earth and died, October 3, 1226.

DECEMBER 15, 1952 My own experience with people over these last five years is that even the best and most undeniable explanations why it would be an advantage to stop some unpleasant manifestation in themselves do not lead to change. Put like this, it is as though the true motive force is left out. On the other hand if logical explanations about the practical advantage of becoming free of negative emotions are combined with the super-logical explanations about the possibility of their transmutation into something quite new and incommensurable, then something really begins to move in people. In other words, without the idea of the miraculous the system does not work; but with this idea it can and does.

The miraculous in relation to negative emotions begins with the idea of second conscious shock*—the transformation of negative emotions into positive ones. It begins for me with Ouspensky's saying that if we had no negative emotions, we would have no chance of development, so they would have to be invented. They are our own inexhaustible raw material for transmuting into that divine energy which otherwise is incommensurable with our logical efforts.

I remember Ouspensky's saying that first and second conscious shock do not come in chronological succession; that in order to work on the first, self-remembering, you already have to be working successfully on the second, actually transmuting negative emotions. In my personal experience this is true, possible and essential.

AUGUST 9, 1953 I can't help looking back at all those years of Ouspensky's work between the wars as *preparation*—preparation for something that was actually conceived in the end, and by virtue of which all our work and possibilities were transformed. That was the time of sowing and cultivating the soil, this is the time of harvest. Many of the methods and attitudes of the time, it seems to me, had inevitably to be cold, harsh and even in a sense negative. Such methods and attitudes now seem to be outdated by the very achievement which they helped to make possible.

Two very clear examples were in the teaching about negative emotions and imagination. All the emphasis was on not expressing negative emotions, and on the *dangers* of imagination. Probably this was all that was possible at that time. But it is extraordinary how all our people here are unanimous in feeling that the *transformation* of negative emotions direct into affection and understanding has now been made possible for us. Also that intentional imagination, aided by laws and understanding, is one of our chief ways toward the realisation of new states and new possibilities, both individually and for the Work as a whole. Further, this very fundamental change of attitude has come to be linked in all our minds with the idea of 'abandoning the system' and 'reconstructing everything'. In other words, with the entry of the miraculous.

JULY 17, 1954 Loose talking always has bad effects—most of all upon those who talk. People should learn only to talk about our work when it is necessary, and then to talk discreetly; to do this requires understanding and more than a touch of self-remembering*. In general, the methods of the group, its intimate affairs and the work of its individual members should never be discussed outside the group. And if ideas are talked of, they should be put into the speakers' own language, not in the terminology used in meetings—for that will ensure that the speaker thinks at least twice before he utters. It is quite reasonable, quite normal. Only we have to become fully reasonable and normal to realise this.

JULY 17, 1954 One has to realise that the short-term misunderstandings and amusements to which our work gives rise are not so important as all that. We have to learn to act honestly and sincerely, and realise that the results do not lie in our hands. Things which look very unpleasant and distressing when seen against the background of a week, may appear very different when thought of against a year, ten years, or a century. And we are working in long time.

NOVEMBER 9, 1954 To talk badly about this Work is to separate oneself from it for a very long time, perhaps for ever. And certain opportunities don't repeat.

DECEMBER 10, 1954 There is so much doubt and self-doubt in the world that it is not easy to remain unperturbed in one's own vision of certainty. When we have certainty, we must actively project it to others, or they will gradually nibble it away from us.

MARCH 12, 1955 Today the truth can be written more clearly and simply than has ever been possible before. And if it is really sincere and unpretentious it will not arouse opposition.

What we affirm we strengthen. If we affirm opposition and misunderstanding, we ourselves feed it. Our work must contain no internal hesitation and lack of faith which undermines its strength. We must be content to state with conviction what we know and believe. The way people take it is not our business.

INVISIBILITY

JANUARY 31, 1950 Becoming visible, becoming known by a name, limits possibilities. The use of a name is almost a kind of magic—it burdens the fate of the person concerned with all the things, both good and bad, which arise from the use of his name. And one knows that the immense unlimited possibilities which Ouspensky opened up were made possible precisely because he had always kept himself invisible and nearly nameless.

JUNE 1, 1951 The more real work, real development, real experiment there is, the more effective the screen to cover the attempt of a few to disappear somewhere else. If a man does all he has to, one day he can disappear, leaving a vortex of power in his place about which all the rest will rightly revolve. And he will no longer be seen.

MAY 13, 1952 Right things must be done quietly and the more invisibly, the better.

SEPTEMBER 9, 1952 It may be right to arrange special times for ourselves, but it should be really invisible. One thing which always creates strain is the impression that someone is 'doing' more than others.

FEBRUARY 22, 1953 The question of individual name and reputation is very paradoxical. While one is acting by oneself in ordinary life, one's name is like a sign or symbol of all the karma, good and bad, that one has accumulated during one's life or lives. For this reason it is important to 'guard' one's name, as the Egyptians realised, and indeed as every honourable person realises.

But when one begins to be absorbed in the work of a school* or even of a prepared group, then it is no longer a question of individual karma. It becomes necessary to play roles or perform tasks that are in no way deserved by the individual karma, but are required by the school. If the person takes the results of playing these roles personally, and uses them to heighten his own name or reputation, then it is a kind of deception or stealing which can deeply damage his own development. For this reason one must learn to act invisibly, impersonally. Or, if it is necessary to use one's name, one gives it as one would give work or money, without trying to profit personally by the results.

On other occasions it might be necessary to lend one's individual name as a kind of propitiation. But then the person who bore the name disappears or becomes invisible, leaving his name as a sacrifice. Who could be more invisible than Judas Iscariot?

The chief thing in esoteric work is to know how to act invisibly—'Let not thy left hand know what thy right hand doeth.' If one has really learnt how to act invisibly then it does not matter if one uses one's name or not, because it indicates that a certain illusion regarding personal fame is dead. And that is the key to all the rest.

FEBRUARY 20, 1956 I have a very strong feeling that the Work is not ours, but comes from above us, and that for this reason the more invisible we remain as personal individuals the better.

ATTENTION

OCTOBER 27, 1949 Attention has the power of holding in a fixed field certain invisible matter or energy in molecular* state, which without attention diffuses indefinitely.

This matter in molecular state has all kinds of powers of penetration, indefinite expansion and contraction, and so on, which of course the physical organism lacks; and in certain circumstances, through 'thinking—visualising—sensing' exercises done with great attention, the 'experience' of this matter in molecular state can, I think, be communicated back to the understanding. Certainly laws* can be studied in this way with very interesting results.

As I say, I think this idea that *attention controls matter in molecular state* is of greatest possible importance to us, and leads to many interesting things indeed.

JUNE 13, 1951 The real food of 'inner impressions' all depends on one being able to divide one's attention and observe what goes on within—one's thoughts, emotions, hopes, fears and health—objectively; that is, *as though they were not one's own.* When that happens one may derive as much understanding, or more, from observing the world within as from observing the world without. Indeed, each will explain the other. But this is only possible with self-remembering*.

SEPTEMBER 12, 1952 It is strange when one has to hold new understandings without being able to speak about them or confirm them with others. But it is also useful. One has to learn to make them permeate one's whole being, one's whole mass instead of rising to the surface of one's throat and tongue. These understandings represent higher energy: and one has to learn by physical attention to *deposit* this energy throughout one's body. Difficult to explain.

JANUARY 10, 1953 Some people take in outside impressions very easily but just as quickly pass them out again—in talking, laughing, all the contacts of life. So nothing can accumulate within. They need inner impressions to fix a point of growth.

Other people's centre of gravity is much more on inner impressions, perceptions, understandings. But unless these inner impressions are constantly aerated with outer impressions, they begin to ferment, turn to dreams and fumes. For such people a constant flow of outer impressions is *absolutely necessary*. Without them, they get more and more separated from other people and from life.

The whole thing is that the inner and outer shall balance, harmonise. What good if one can do everything, be everything, without understanding why? But also, what good if one understands everything, and can do nothing, communicate nothing? And this doesn't only mean explaining to other people what one feels, but also being sensitive to what they feel even if they don't explain.

SEPTEMBER 16, 1954 I am very interested in the effects of the *continued* performance of music or prayers on earth. Interesting to think, for example, that the Lord's Prayer has become a kind of permanent murmur for mankind during the last fifteen hundred years. And certain kinds of chanting must have been equally continuous over the whole continent of Europe for two or three centuries. Imagine today also how all the surroundings of man are continuously soaked in music of one kind or another, from gramophone and radio. This must very deeply effect the molecular constitution of his world, the landscape of his soul.

MARCH 2, 1956 It is good when people in a group begin to break down their separateness, their private reservations which keep them stuck in the same place. The next step is to learn to work together. Probably it should be either creating or serving —painting, sculpture, crafts, building; or on the other hand teaching, helping the poor or the sick, trying to bring hope to the darkest corners of life. These are the two ways in which people transcend themselves, escape from their own troubles into a larger world.

If one can find a work which combines the two, that is best of all. Any real work must be a response to some need in the surroundings of the group itself. It cannot be invented. People must learn to see the real needs in the world around them, from the point of view of the Work.

We must not forget that the soul grows by being given away. What does this mean for us, where we stand? Attention directs the matter of the soul. If we really *give* our attention to others—to their needs, their hopes, their problems—we are beginning to give our soul. And that is how the soul grows. If one tries to make a soul to keep, it withers to nothing.

If it is too shocking for people to think about *giving* the soul, let them think about the idea of projection. The quality, intensity and harmony of what we project is closely connected with the growth of the soul. And we must learn to project consciously, that is with attention and will.

To do this we have to stop thinking about ourselves. What prevents us from developing the power of projection is self-centredness, introspection, preoccupation with one's own imagination, and self-pity, all this illusion which turns our creative force in upon itself.

I think there has been a lot of imagination about this. When people begin this work, they have to be told to observe themselves, study the machine they have to work with. Because they never took their own instrument, its possibilities and its limitations, into account before. But that doesn't mean they have to go on thinking about themselves all the rest of their lives. If you want to study micro-biology, you first have to study your microscope, find out its magnifying power, adjustments, illumination, factor of distortion and so on. But when you've done that, you put all your attention onto your slides, and forget you are looking through a microscope altogether. Then your real discoveries begin.

Focus on self-study belongs to a definite stage. If it goes on too long, people become professional students, than which nothing is more useless. So they should begin transferring their focus of attention from themselves to their real life-work, whatever it may be. And the sooner they realise what their life-work is going to be, the sooner they will come to reality.

After that, all self-observation becomes incidental—simply registering what helps or hinders what one has to do.

MARCH 5, 1956 We have been studying the history of art and culture. People need to look more into the depth of time, in order to escape from preoccupation with themselves and the little movements of their minds. I think this is one of the chief reasons why we have to go on learning. If one does not give one's attention to what is really interesting, one gives one's attention to oneself, which gets one nowhere.

REQUIREMENTS AND CIRCUMSTANCES

DECEMBER 25, 1948 Perhaps the most difficult and important thing is to learn to wait. And when one asks oneself what one is waiting for, one begins to realise that it is for a moment of stillness, without attachment to the past or future. For in such a moment all kinds of exercises and perceptions become possible which are never available when one is hurrying into the future or out of the past.

It seems to us that the important times are those when much is happening, much is required, and one is hypnotised by motion. It may be quite different. Now I begin to feel that all that is important comes in quietness and waiting; and that activity should be only the working out, the digesting and putting forth of what one learned, so that one may become empty again to receive more.

FEBRUARY 18, 1949 Evidently many ideas and new perceptions can come to us, if physical and emotional strains and the motion of the mind are quieted. But it is not quite tension which is the obstacle. It is more than that—something like the whole momentum of life, identification with the rushing forward of time. Difficult to explain. Sometimes it happens that a great ordeal, or a long fast, or having a baby, breaks this momentum, and then all kinds of new impressions enter that could never catch up when one was tearing into the future like an express train.

I often think of the last years with Ouspensky. He would have two or three people sit with him, not doing anything, just sitting, smoking, occasionally making a remark, drinking a glass of wine, for hours on end. At first it was very difficult—one racked one's brains what to say, how to start a conversation, thought of all kinds of imaginary duties elsewhere. Many people could never bear it. But after a while, these became the most interesting times of all. One began to feel—everything is possible in *this* moment, let the past and future take care of itself. Some kind of momentum slowed down, and sometimes quite new ideas, a quite new connection with time and one's surroundings, seemed to form. One was shown what it meant to be more free.

Of course one cannot create such situations without an Ouspensky. One has to work hard, and play one's role in life, probably without much sitting down. But *innerly* I think it is possible to slow down this momentum, to accept what the *present* brings and live in that. From an intense sense of the present it is possible to feel certain connections in the past and future. If one is not established in the present, then one is nowhere and nothing is possible.

Really it is only *involuntary* tension which prevents this. *Deliberate* tension seems to be exactly what helps prepare for relaxation. The Movements* we used to do, some yogi exercises, probably some Indian dancing, are from one point of view based on intense deliberate tension of certain parts of the body, certain functions, which afterwards become relaxed and thus channels for finer energy which can never penetrate them in the ordinary way. It is the same with emotion. Involuntary emotional strain is only exhausting. But the deliberate undertaking of emotionally difficult tasks, *understanding why*, can certainly lead to a higher kind of emotional understanding.

All the difference in the world is between voluntary and involuntary. Two ideas were sometimes spoken of: First, 'Sacrifice your suffering', and then much later, the idea of 'intentional suffering'. The first refers to involuntary, and the second to voluntary. But one must get rid of the first before one can come to the second, and all that can be bought in that way.

Probably there is some similar principle in sex. But sex is so subtle, so delicate, so quickly influenced by other functions, that theory doesn't help much. I think one thing Ouspensky said covers everything else: 'Never let anything negative come near sex.'

FEBRUARY 16, 1950 'Food, air and impressions' were deliberately put together because esoteric physiology explains that these are in fact the three different kinds of food upon which man lives. And that each of these different kinds of 'food' is taken in and undergoes a process of digestion and refinement within him. Only whereas the full digestion of material food by the body is arranged mechanically by nature, the full digestion of impressions depends upon man's own efforts and particularly upon his learning to remember himself. The possible end-product of the digestion of impressions is a much higher matter than the final product of either food or air, and upon it, all balanced development depends. For this reason in our system much more attention is given to the use of impressions than to special diets or special breathing, which by themselves may even be dangerous and harmful. In our way it is said that all work must begin from normal conditions, from what is most normal and natural for the man in question.

MARCH 21, 1950 It is extraordinary what doors the abandonment of talk, or words, seems to open—doors that talk prevented one from ever suspecting. First one has to get everything one can—and that is very much—from the right use of words; then when one has got from them all they can give, one must be brave enough to throw all that overboard and begin again in quite a different way.

NOVEMBER 16, 1951 Sometimes, by 'letting go' we allow some 'grace' to enter by another channel, which all our mental efforts have hitherto kept out. Stillness is a quality of the heart. We must not expect to find it among the doubts of the mind—it is the mind which must make way for it.

AUGUST 24, 1952 I think participation in life is very right and part of a pattern. While a new direction is being formed in one, one must feel oneself pulling away from life all the time, even one may have to live out of life in some special circumstances. But when the new direction is really established, and one's inner life is permanently magnetised to a new pole, then I think one has to go back into life—really in, without reservations, much more deeply and intimately than one ever did before. For it is in life that the Work is done, that results can be measured, objectively, at any rate in the fourth way*.

And gradually, without quite knowing how it happened, one begins to see everything—one's own life included—against a larger background. Cause and effect ceases to be a question of before or after, and becomes a kind of leavening of the whole mixture. And the more one lives in relation to one's whole life, the less any part of it—past or future—can be kept separate from any other. The town to which the traveller goes for the first time always lay at the end of that particular road, but after he has visited it, he can send back the news from there to every village and inn along the road.

AUGUST 24, 1952 Assisi is certainly presided over by St. Francis, but a pretty tough Francis, with a power proportionate to the fears he was freed from.

Looked at from here and now some of the traditionally saintly things look less extraordinary, others more so. All this about the birds and animals seems simply like the reaction of a man who has become normal against the background of an age which regarded the whole animal kingdom as rather diabolic. But the fact that nothing seemed impossible to him and the more impossible things looked, the more urgently they had to be done—this has the genuine ring. Embracing the leper, yes.

NOVEMBER 15, 1952 People who have a particular kind of sensitiveness have their own special advantages and their own special disadvantages in this Work. All of us have to grow more balanced, more normal, in preparation for work to become supernormal. In the general work towards more balance between the different sides of ourselves any special difficulty will fit into its proper place. I doubt if it can or should be dealt with as something separate in itself.

JUNE 10, 1953 One must not try to cling on to opportunities which have come, however pleasant and comforting. For that is the way to kill them. Let good things go without regret. Then better ones may come.

MAY 31, 1953 There must always be Friday evenings and Monday mornings and we must slog along through them as best we can. I don't think there is a world in which it is always weekend in any dimension, except perhaps in the seventh!

It seems to me that one is never depleted by real contact with others. When something can flow through one to other people, one feels full of life. It is when something grows stagnant that exhaustion sets in.

AUGUST 1, 1953 To smoke or not to smoke can be an interesting experiment. In discovering the enormous power of motor mechanicalness we discover a great secret. At a certain moment at the time of Ouspensky's death I felt, among many other experiences, that I was like a mechanical toy condemned to go on moving till the spring had run down. Then immobility, death. Moving centre seemed to me to be the root of our mechanicalness, and I realised that all beginning of consciousness depends upon a certain 'stop', as described in *In Search of the Miraculous*.

At this same time I noticed one day that Ouspensky was showing us an exercise that would demonstrate this mechanicalness, and give us the means of overcoming it. But he did the exercise without words or explanations; it was almost invisible.

The exercise was as follows: One sits comfortably in a chair. Then for a definite time—say half an hour—one moves, slightly and naturally. *But without stopping for a single moment.* For example, one puts out one's right hand to take a cigarette, one lights it, crosses one's legs, rubs one's cheek, turns one's head, knocks the ash off the cigarette into the ashtray etc. etc. *But all in slow but continuous movement.*

After half an hour of this one begins to realise the true nature of movement. And at the end, for a short time, one has the possibility of remaining completely still, without any movement at all. From this immobility further realisations can come.

FEBRUARY 11, 1955 Contact with the earth and with simple people is necessary for us. Apart from what they receive, their contact refreshes us, gives us rest and security. And when people begin to work seriously, and begin to feel the tremendous strain of what has to be done, it is very important that they learn to rest in a new way. In order to work with all one has, one must learn to rest with all one has, too. 'Earthing' has something to do with rest. But we must learn to work with all kinds of people—particularly worldly people, people who have come to decent values through struggle with worldly conditions. For they are better prepared than many dreamers.

August 16, 1955 When we are ill, our first duty is to get well —and we do that by resting, doing the things we like, opening our pores to what is natural and beautiful, and avoiding boredom at all costs.

October 24, 1955 It is true that the pressure of new experiences, new demands and new efforts makes us 'explosive'. But we must realise that this explosiveness is only a physical phenomenon, and treat it as such. It is the body adjusting itself to a new rhythm of life—so we have to give it the opportunity of getting rid of its bile in ways that are not harmful, by exercise, dancing, shouting at the sky from the top of the nearest mountain, or whatever. In any case, we must never imagine that it is *ourselves* that are explosive, never imagine that there is anything wrong with our soul, when it is only the body. Everyone must find his own personal way of resting, by his speciality, his hobby, the movies or other more mystical ways of escaping from mental or muscular tension. He who does not know how to rest cannot carry on. *It is important.*

SELF-REMEMBERING

JUNE 3, 1950 When one begins to see that one can only begin to remember oneself for seconds at a time, it seems negligible. But what one must understand is that it is difficult exactly because it is the beginning of a *new state* for us, the key to a *new world*. If it were easy and if results came more quickly it could not have the importance which it has.

Exactly for this reason it is impossible to say how long it will take to reach self-remembering. How long will it take to reach Mexico? Some people could go there in a day, some in a month, some in a year, some in ten years, but most people never, because there is no reason for them to go there. So with self-remembering. Only for those who want it very much and try very much, *time* is necessary—years, many years. And even if they do get what they understand by self-remembering they will see that beyond that, infinite new distances and new meanings open up, and that the achievement of one stage of it is only the beginning of another.

NOVEMBER 16, 1951 The inner question which interests me now is the idea of what can be third force in self-remembering. We have been told that every phenomenon is produced by three forces, and that two alone can give no result. And the double-headed arrow has over many years shown us clearly what two of these factors in self-remembering are. But in the presence of what third power must these two forces find themselves for this new state to be really consummated and give what it should? I think this can lead us to quite new things.

JANUARY 26, 1953 Stendhal wrote to his most intimate friend: 'I consider there is nothing ridiculous in dying in the street—provided one doesn't do it on purpose.' Exactly a year later he did so—presumably not on purpose. Ouspensky once said that having a sense of humour about oneself was the unprepared man's way of self-remembering.

June 25, 1953 In all experiments and efforts and disappointments, we must never forget the idea of self-remembering. No matter whether one is scientifically or mystically inclined, whether one finds oneself stuck in one's old life, or in the middle of quite new experiences, *this* provides one's compass, this will show one the direction in which to go and prevent one from ever becoming lost.

June 26, 1953 When true self-remembering comes, one does not want to alter oneself, or others; one somehow rises above their weaknesses and one's own. There can be no blame anywhere. One swallows what is, and becomes free.

December 3, 1954 We mustn't let the effort to self-remember slip into introspection. If one feels oneself an intensely living being in an intensely living world, the whole penetrated by living Divinity, feels what it means to give, to feel, to collect simultaneously, gradually the taste of it will penetrate deeply into one, and make a constant longing for it.

February 7, 1955 I feel that distress is a quality in being which will be evoked by anything unexpected. Shall we not reach a state where by self-remembering we accept what is, and distress is no longer in us? We must, we can.

OTHER PEOPLE

MAY 1948 To impose our own feelings or ideas on others is absolutely wrong. There can be no right relation to others but bringing out their own real and deepest purpose and understanding.

JUNE 22, 1948 I saw the other day that the phrase 'One cannot do', which became a blasphemous denial of all possibilities, is really only half of an aphorism, which expresses many laws in a compressed way. The full aphorism should be: 'One cannot do, but it can be done by three*.'

AUGUST 15, 1948 It is probably the pressure of other people which pushes one forward and shows clearly what one has to do. And it seems very important to learn not to shirk this pressure, even in the smallest things, but to respond to its indications and lead those who exert it into the fulfilment of a larger plan. It is always important to remember that this pressure, although it may often take foolish forms, represents the desire to grow of a certain body of people who have already been sorted out by a higher test than we could ever arrange. And it is this total desire for growth, if it can be rightly harnessed, which can raise us to the point where we make contact with direction from above.

Afterwards, it is the contacts that one failed to make or respond to, *when it was possible*, that one regrets, realising that these omissions can never really be repaired later. If we leave the contact till too late, the moment will have passed and in a few weeks all the pawns have moved and stand in a quite different relation to each other.

One can never absolve oneself when someone takes a wrong course *through one's own omission*. I feel very strongly that the negative attitude which became attached to and perverted the idea that 'One cannot do' has to be countered by the idea that 'it may be done through me'. Anyone who has really felt the idea that one can do nothing in the same realisation must see that very great things are required by higher powers to be done through whatever instruments are available. And that this idea requires *much more* from individuals than does the ordinary belief that they can arrange their own destinies.

JANUARY 31, 1950 I now see very clearly that not only must one give to people what they ask, but also that one must not give them what they do not ask for, nor before they ask it. The attempt always defeats its own end.

FEBRUARY 10, 1950 There are two complementary laws in our work. The first is, what a man asks sincerely, you must give him, if you can. The second is, *only* what he asks and only *when* he asks can anything be given at all. Any attempt to break this law always produces wrong results. That is why I also have to ask: 'What do you want to know?' And you have to find out. For nobody but yourself can answer this question, and if anybody else tries to answer it for you, run from him as fast as you can.

FEBRUARY 22, 1950 The beginning of a new attitude, a new understanding of the world seems to lie in the feeling that we are an integral, an organic part of it, that it pervades us, and that all that we can see or study or imagine outside is also contained in little within us. I think this feeling, when it really penetrates, of itself begins to melt this strange false feeling of 'I', of separateness, of exclusion, from which we suffer. If we are excluded from the best things in the universe it is because we choose to be, because we imagine ourselves like that—not because it is so.

MAY 18, 1950 More and more I become astonished how similar ideas—which seem to derive from big school*—are expressed simultaneously by people who apparently have no connection with each other or with anything and yet the timing of the release of certain ideas at many different points and in many different forms is so beautiful that one can't but suspect some school planning behind it.

To me this is the natural outcome of the understanding that

one cannot do. When one really begins to feel this one comes to a kind of dead stop—one can't do anything of oneself, and one knows that everything one tries to do of oneself can *only* end in fiasco. Where to turn? One begins to long for school and to fall in with school aims and school laws as the only certain security, the only meaning, the only escape from the hopeless effort to do when one knows one can't do.

August 28, 1950 There are some people who can go straight there, and quite suddenly see how everything works—in themselves and in everything. But then they return with a bump and have to continue in ordinary life, amid ordinary resistances and ordinary densities of matter, and among people who have ordinary capacities, but not that one.

How to make what you perceive *there* comprehensible *here*? How to introduce it sufficiently quietly, reasonably and undeniably into ordinary life that people will not run away, but will be attracted and convinced? That was what Ouspensky knew so supremely well. He said you have to move in a certain way with cats, or they'll run away, and in a certain way with bees, or they'll sting you. That's how it is with human beings too. You have to learn how not to startle them, particularly if you've seen something they have not seen.

It's most unsatisfactory to be here one moment—then hey presto—you're there, and hey presto, you're back again, without quite knowing what happened. And very irritating for your friends. So the whole thing is to build a bridge between here and there, a good solid one.

So listen quietly to what everybody says, and see how much fits in with what you've seen yourself, see what expands it, explains it from another side. Gradually, the bigger picture will emerge, the picture of the whole bridge going up. When you see that, many difficulties with people will vanish.

There is something which may sometimes seem like fire, fire which cleanses without consuming, unites without destroying, which licks upward through everything and yet is never seen—but we have called it electronic* matter, which sounds much more respectable, and is just as accurate. It looks as though we have to learn to tell things in ordinary language, which won't frighten people, which won't look too fantastic and unreasonable.

It is not so much that it is forbidden to refer to certain things, but that one must not refer to them in language unsuitable to those one is talking to. One must not describe something intellectually to a person who lives in instinct. For you will only discredit what you speak about, and get your head broken into the bargain. So one has to learn to speak in the language the person one is talking to can understand.

NOVEMBER 24, 1951 We used to talk very much about the idea 'one cannot do' and it came to me that this is only half an esoteric axiom, the other half being: 'but all can be done by three'. The great freedom seems to lie in giving up the idea that one can *do*, that is, produce all three forces from inside oneself at will, and understand that *it will be done*, if we rightly play our part as *one* force in the triad and learn how to evoke and acknowledge the hidden presence of the others.

DECEMBER 12, 1951 I believe that at a certain point healing others, physically, emotionally, mentally, or all three, becomes obligatory on anyone who wishes to develop, and that if this element is left out a wrong turning can be taken.

DECEMBER 12, 1951 I have no wish to prevent those who so desire from reading any book, because I believe that a healthy judgement, given all evidence, will form its own conclusions. And that any prohibitions or suppressions must either warp this judgement or make it work on incomplete knowledge.

JANUARY 24, 1952 Each person who tries to take part in school work has to develop his own method, has to find in himself his own inner law, and work with others according to that law. My own inner law will not permit me to demand of others anything that they do not desire to do of their own free will; my own personal 'way' does not permit arbitrary rules. It is connected with trying to make people see all sides, in the belief that if they do, healthy judgement will draw its own right conclusions.

JANUARY 27, 1952 If one tries to explain to other people what one has learned, one finds that such explanations are only right and successful if they are the result of what those people ask of one, demand of one, really want to know of themselves. If one explains something to them before they ask, they will not hear it, and one will be disappointed.

Everything happens by right combination of three forces—active, passive, mediating. In the first stages, it is he who wishes to learn who must be active, who must force the one who knows a little more to explain. If he who knows more is active, that is, if he tries to explain first, the wrong result or no result is produced.

Only one must answer by what one understands, from principles certainly, but according to one's understanding of them—from one's *own* experience, one's *own* examples.

JULY 16, 1952 There always remains the problem of how people can communicate with each other *accurately* and hand on tradition about the relation of ideas, about cosmology and technique. What Ouspensky used to call 'the problem of new language'. In recent months it has appeared to us more and more that the best means might be by symbols, provided that they are true ones and rightly organised. People have a great resistance to accepting a new and exact meaning of an old word, and quite new words are unpleasant in that they have none of the overtones and associations which enrich old ones. But symbols could be their own argument and explanation. It always seems to have been arranged like that among schools which left traces in architecture, painting or poetry.

JULY 16, 1952 The reaction of simple people, peasants and workmen, to a direct expression of certain laws and ideas and harmony interests me very much. They learn by physical work and loyalty, and they teach one in the same way.

AUGUST 6, 1952 There is intentional and recognised hypnotism and accidental and unrecognised hypnotism. It is the absolute duty of everyone who attempts to guide others to abstain as much as possible from producing these effects, and it is equally the duty of the apprentice always to struggle against fear and fascination in himself. Ouspensky never allowed us to become fascinated, and his mere presence precluded fear. But there were circumstances in which we had to judge for ourselves on the basis of these principles and with the memory of his example. Such circumstances constituted a test of our understanding.

SEPTEMBER 11, 1952 I think the most important thing, when people ask, is to be sincere, as sincere as possible. Not hide anything, not invent anything. Say the answer which comes unhindered from the heart. People recognise simple sincerity, when arguments don't touch them, evasions annoy them.

NOVEMBER 10, 1952 The best way to learn is to teach, provided that the one who teaches is the deepest 'I' that really knows.

JANUARY 3, 1953 I remember Ouspensky speaking very interestingly once in New York about sincerity. We think we have only to decide to be and we can be. But sincerity has to be learnt, slowly and painfully. Takes long long time. And when one finds sincerity on one level, one realises that there is another completely different level of sincerity hidden beneath. At Ouspensky's last meetings at Colet Gardens in '48, he reached the deepest level I ever met in living man.

JANUARY 3, 1953 New life streams down on us, is all around us, we drown in it. All that is necessary is that we become empty or porous, for it to permeate us. As long as one really remembers this, I think one may speak to others, if it seems right. The moment one forgets it, danger enters.

FEBRUARY 25, 1954 It is clear to me that one of the conditions for development is to learn to work selflessly and with understanding for the general good. Those who do so, begin to become free, whether they are in organised school or not. And in turn this selfless understanding work—to improve material conditions, to make education available, to heal, mentally or physically—creates conditions where more people can meet the chance of real school. It all fits together on the biggest scale. The process of healing is necessary *preparation* for the process of regeneration.

OCTOBER 11, 1954 It is true that energy can be connected with the idea of giving and receiving. He who learns how to give away wisely all he has received will never have to worry about shortage of energy. In order to make a big jump, it looks as though we have to bequeath all our possessions—of knowledge, skill, understanding, habit, loyalty, affection. But as in making a will, one has to give away each quality to someone who can receive it and use it. Then one is free for new tasks. Ouspensky did this completely before he died. We have to get the habit now. Then we can begin receiving on a different scale.

FEBRUARY 25, 1955 No one need worry about fondness for the human race. Only we must make it always more real, more our own. We mustn't let it become second hand. Would the Saints be Saints, if they hadn't been much more fond of the human race than the rest of us, first hand?

OCTOBER 1, 1955 There are so many ways in which fundamental laws can be expressed. But for me the one thing important is that we go on and on, penetrating always deeper and higher to more simplicity, more sincerity, more honesty. We must never give words and forms and theories time to crystallise around us.

'Move, move, you must move from the place where you are.' To me those words of Ouspensky's last week become constantly more urgent. For I know that it is now made *possible* for us to move, and that we are helped to do so if we really wish it. We can be given the answer to any question if we ask it innerly and sincerely and are prepared to abide by the answer we receive.

OCTOBER 3, 1955 We must teach people by asking them, not telling them. Then there will be no resistance. We should try to draw the truth out of them, not inject it into them. If they do not respond, it is not our fault; but if they do, we will learn much.

October 12, 1955 If people do not express their deepest doubts and speak sincerely, no one can help them. They must change their impulse to run away into an honest effort to overcome their obstacles. Otherwise they are preferring their doubts to freedom from them.

November 2, 1955 We must learn to speak more and more simply. That is good for the people we talk to and good for us. We must be simple, honest, sincere, and open to what others bring us. The rest is not in our hands.

People are very preoccupied with words. One tries to describe something freshly, in different words, and they think the bottom has fallen out of the universe. You say: 'You must eat to live,' and they say they understand. Then you say: 'Come and have lunch.' And they exclaim: 'What! I thought we were supposed to eat!'

January 11, 1956 We must try to be kind and sincere and truthful. It is no good to be kind without being sincere. It is no good to be sincere without being kind. And neither are any good unless we try to connect them with truth. It means one has to be much more simple and open, remembering oneself and forgetting oneself in one.

February 10, 1956 My experience is that one can say anything to people, provided one says it simply and straight, not critically, but with affection as a statement of fact. They react immediately to sincerity and warmth, curl up and go dumb at anything like irony or criticism if it contains the slightest intention to hurt. I think one can say things that touch people very closely provided one waits for the moment when there is warmth and confidence, and then does not say it de haut en bas, but simply as another poor devil like themselves—only a poor devil who has learnt to take neither his own reactions nor the other's too seriously.

MARCH 19, 1956 Our work is to accept and not to impose. Everything that fills us with ourselves is not work, but vanity. It is better to do nothing than to act from pride and call it work. We have to attain harmony. This means to be oneself. But it also means to accept others, respect them, learn from them, become connected with something higher.

APRIL 6, 1956 Our work is the development of whatever is positive and constructive in ourselves and in our companions. But how? By demanding that others be positive inevitably provokes a wave of resistance and negativeness. It is nobody's fault; it is a law.

We must remember the action of three forces in different order. If the active force begins, the passive force unavoidably reacts, and the result of the struggle is a meaningless average. This happens in all ordinary life. This process has nothing to do with the mysterious order of forces that bring regeneration, which begins with the third—with understanding, with tolerance, with invisible help. When we know the taste of this other order of forces which begins not by imposition but by acceptance, we will find that by it everything becomes easy. And the positiveness that we are trying to demand by force already is there.

CORRECTING MISTAKES

FEBRUARY 25, 1949 I am sure that it is in some way an esoteric principle that records have to be 'made right'. It is not a question of hiding mistakes or unpleasantness or anything like that. But if someone in the play acts outside of character, so to speak, the record has to correct it. The text of the play has to be more perfect than the play itself. How this can be is practically impossible to say. The New Testament must be the perfect example: *everything* is right.

SEPTEMBER 4, 1949 I have a very strong understanding that it is only possible to move from one's position by first paying off all one's debts. And since one is in fact indebted to everyone one ever knew, it means that one has to put *every* relation right —in actuality, if that is still possible, or innerly in one's mind if it is not. Evidently right prayer might be one way of doing this.

It struck me very much how Ouspensky, in speaking about his parents, relations or old friends, always recalled their possibilities, their best sides, what they might become, and never recalled anything negative or unpleasant about them. This also seems connected with the same idea—making people better than they are.

To anyone who spoke about higher states of consciousness, or positive emotions, or experiences of higher man, Ouspensky used to answer: 'Later on you will see . . . ' or 'Not yet . . .' or 'We will come to that later . . .' or 'When you reach such a point, you . . .' always with the understanding that the person could and would eventually come to the highest possibilities. In this way he made it possible for them to do so. And in the same way, without one knowing how it happened, he took away fear, the fear of failure.

OCTOBER 5, 1949 I had the feeling that one must go carefully through one's life and pay one's debts. And this seemed somehow to involve begging forgiveness of everyone one ever knew; for after all, we are indebted in one way or another to all people we met, we have wronged them in some way, large or small, and it is we who must seek to be forgiven our debts, if we are to become free to move.

NOVEMBER 3, 1949 Remorse is a very strange thing. If one could imagine remorse without any negative emotion attached to it—from that one might learn very much indeed.

But these moments which we call by this name are usually when we see ourselves and the results of our past actions without meaning to. I think we must mean to, intend to. We must try to remember ourselves in time, remember our lives in detail. By real and intentional remembering we shall see the results of our past actions and attitudes, see to whom we are indebted. Eventually no one can move unless his debts are paid. But before being paid, they must be seen and acknowledged. And this is possible only through self-remembering*.

NOVEMBER 24, 1950 Don't worry about past mistakes. Only take pains to pay them off in a small way whenever opportunity arises. Clear up old misunderstandings, be natural and easy with people you once shocked. Ten small debts paid off are worth more than one large one. Value that which comes naturally, value work that looks small-scale. In this way trust is established. When trust has grown up, then you can tell people about big things. But these other things can only be communicated in an atmosphere of trust. And trust grows slowly—out of small things.

It is not only what we see for ourselves. It is also becoming absorbed into the body of school, the class. Then what we have seen can pass to others, and what they have seen can pass to us. This is the secret of school. But to be absorbed means that the more shocking corners must be rubbed off, trust established. For trust is the medium in which school works.

JUNE 7, 1951 Personally, I think it is good from time to time to come back to a really deep study of the *meaning* of the Lord's Prayer, particularly in relation to oneself, one's own life. Sometimes this is very shocking. For instance, how awful to have repeated again and again: 'Forgive us our trespasses as we forgive them that trespass against us.' And then suddenly to find that one has not forgiven them at all, but on the contrary constantly blamed them for everything unpleasant that happened.

I remember when I was about six or seven, my mother was teaching me the Lord's Prayer, and when we got to this point, I suddenly burst out: 'But that means that if we don't forgive people, we are asking not to be forgiven!' Maybe that small boy was quite right.

If we could really forgive, we could really move—there would be nothing to stop us.

JUNE 9, 1953 Everything can change in time, without limit, but probably in a certain order, exactly connected with the paying off of karma.

When people are on the right road, probably one should perpetuate only that which belongs to their highest understanding. Something to do with making people out better than they are, writing off their weaker sides. Somehow in this way they are helped and one helps oneself. Rather mysterious.

THE INFLUENCE OF CONSCIOUS MEN

AUGUST 29, 1948 About 'casting pearls before swine'—this is only half an esoteric truth; the other facet is expressed by the parable of the talents.

Perhaps there has been some misunderstanding about what is truly esoteric, or 'influence C' as it was called. 'Influence C' appears to refer to the actual work of higher man upon his intimate pupils—by transmission of knowledge, example, tests, and so on. Ouspensky's direct work on individual people became, if it can be expressed like that, more and more esoteric up to the end. And to the memories of *this* the warning about 'casting pearls before swine' refers very strictly.

On the other hand, the moment knowledge passes out from such a circle, it is no longer esoteric. It changes from influence C to influence B, that is, it ceases to be particular and becomes general. From my point of view, the discussion of Ouspensky's lectures among hundreds of people, over whom he had no close control, both in and out of the Work, meant that they long ago ceased to be esoteric. The proof of this is that ideas began to produce the opposite results from those originally intended—fear of experiment instead of experiment, despair instead of understanding, and so on. For this reason, they had to be reconstructed, as he said.

Now we are left with the *traces* of Ouspensky's teaching and the explanation of principles in the understanding of some hundreds of people. But by natural laws, these traces will become expressed and will filter out into the world in one form or another. And from my point of view they should filter out in this way.

I would even say that, as the parable of the talents explains, each person who has received special knowledge will one day be required to give account of the use he has made of it, the reconstruction or expression he has given to it. This expression will evidently depend on the capacities of each individual concerned. It may be in writing, in art, direct example, service to others, what you will. But I am convinced that every individual understanding of special teaching must leave its appropriate trace somewhere. If no trace is apparent, the understanding must be suspect—for in our experience it is only dreams which leave no trace.

JANUARY 9, 1949 There is something very interesting in the direct connection with simple people. This last link in the chain from higher man through his near pupils, his distant admirers, and on down to the ordinary decent people with whom they come in contact, has always interested me. Somehow it seems necessary to complete the pattern of things; something must flow on from us away to the circumference of life, in order to make room for new understanding and energy to enter us from the centre.

MARCH 13, 1950 I do not think the prohibition of the use of alcohol and tobacco belong to true esotericism, but rather to pseudo-esotericism. For in true esotericism everything depends not so much on what is outwardly done, but upon *how* it is done, for *what reason*, and so on. So that many things which are apparently very innocent, may in reality be most dangerous and unlawful at a certain time and for certain types of people—because they are *mechanical.* While other things and actions of which many people would disapprove may on the contrary be useful and even essential, *if there is meaning and consciousness behind their use.* I only mean to say that in esotericism things are not what they seem.

This is the difference between all books about esotericism—even the best—and the actual work of a teacher. A book has to make generalisations which can supposedly apply to everyone; whereas a teacher treats each pupil differently, according to his type; so that the treatment he gives one type—say to teach him strength and self-control—may be exactly the opposite to that which he gives to another type, who must be taught to become softer, more sensitive and receptive.

JANUARY 24, 1952 C influence, as I understand, always implies the direct action of a man who understands more on another man who understands less. Writings, formulas, diagrams, prayers, can never be in themselves C influence, though the way they are used or given in a particular case by a particular man, may make them so for the moment. Thus C influence is only possible within the organisation of school, though this may have many meanings as yet unrecognised by us.

B influence on the other hand—again as I understand it—consists in the crystallised traces of what was once C influence, recorded, arranged and given out with as much understanding and consciousness as those who received it can muster. The Gospels, the dialogues of Socrates and Buddha, the Tarot pack and so on all seem to fall into this category, though each has its own inner 'level', so to speak.

The delay between the giving of C influence and its conversion into B may be longer and shorter, and the B, once made, may be hidden or withdrawn, even for centuries. Though all this may be much less accidental than we think. But in general the creation of B influence from the traces of C is, I believe, one of the tasks of pupils in certain classes of school, and if they do not do this, some part of school organisation has failed. If they were well prepared and try sincerely, however, I believe they may receive certain help and correction from a master or pupil in a higher class, so that B influence which is ostensibly transmitted by them may not be quite so haphazard or fallacious as one would expect.

Certainly, a kind of general revision and correction of all work put out in the name of the school is done invisibly from above, by methods which we usually attribute to accident, our own cleverness, or the machinations of others.

One thing I feel strongly; that if what was once C influence is kept *without* expression, it does not thereby remain C. On the contrary, it fossilises and dies, blocking the channel of higher communication, leaving one with neither C nor B, nor the possibility of receiving more of either. So that the more of what was once C can be really converted into *suitable* B, the more the way is opened for the reception of *new* C influence direct from a higher level to the individual concerned. For instance, it was only after trying to write down all I could understand about self-remembering in right order for a certain person, that the idea of third force entered in the wake of what had gone before.

My aim is thus to participate in a continuous flow, that passes into us from above, and out of us in one way or another around and about. The moment I cling to some idea as something which cannot be passed on (suitably clothed and adapted and to suitable people, of course) then I immediately create a blockage which prevents new things coming to me. The law of hydraulics in pipes would apply exactly, if only they conveyed that digestion and modification of influence which must be made by the vessel through which it passes.

I do not believe it was accidental that the enneagram* and the idea of self-remembering* were never revealed before, and are now found on the fringe of public knowledge. When things of such power are released from higher school*, they are released with the full knowledge of what is going to happen to them, and in relation to a particular possibility, first for those who receive them 'in school', and second for large numbers of men whom they will later reach without special explanation. I have the strongest possible feeling that the enneagram is an instrument for the understanding of unity[1] deliberately released into the world to balance the prodigious and baffling diversity of knowledge which other aspects of our age have made available. In fact it is the *only* instrument for the understanding of unity proportional to the disintegrative knowledge with which mankind is being overwhelmed. Nobody yet guesses that this one small symbol on paper paves the way for the understanding that mankind must find or destroy itself. Each of us has to work on it, develop it, try to explain, hide or cherish it as best we can, according to our lights. But all of us, and all we can do or not do, are absolutely invisible in relation to the issues involved. Thank God they are in better and greater hands.

JUNE 20, 1953 We want *new* C influence now and constantly. It has been proved that this is possible. In order to make room

[1] Later, when speaking of this idea, R used the word 'harmony' instead of 'unity'. J. C. S.

for it, I believe that what was C influence in the past has gradually to be released into the world as B influence. It seems to me that this is part of the plan and economy of school work. C influence was C influence when it was given and in the circumstances it was given; it does not remain so; and if one tries to preserve it as such, I believe one may prevent the entry of new. At the same time, the order, manner and degree of its release is of very great importance.

TIME

AUGUST 10, 1948 It is clear that the attainment of some higher level by Mr Ouspensky at the time of his death released a very great energy which could touch and affect all those who were innerly attached to him, and which was independent of both space and time. If it is possible to throw aside our very weak and distorted view of time, we may understand that those who have been affected by such energy and such a level of man may continue to draw understanding and direction from that connection though circumstances may separate and isolate them.

SEPTEMBER 4, 1948 Any esoteric work should grow in all dimensions, including time. As the teacher penetrates into higher dimensions, his influence gradually 'spreads' in time. Think of Christ's influence since His life, and also of the strange 'foreshadowing' of His drama, cast into earlier times. How strange it would have been for His disciples, after the crucifixion, to join Apollonius of Tyana because Christ was 'dead'. Their business was to make His work grow in time, to prepare people to come to Him 'through time'. And one of the strangest things about it is that to those who think with ordinary ideas of time, all this must appear 'imagination', 'fantasy', and so on.

OCTOBER 27, 1948 The other thing I feel is absolutely essential, is that we must make every effort to break our usual ideas of time. Sometimes it seems to me that this is the chief illusion of all, and becoming free of it our chief preparation. Try to think of different speeds of time, of time passing faster and faster, or slower and slower, of time going backwards, of parallel times, of time coexisting or standing still, of all these different motions of time going on simultaneously in different parts of the universe. I mean, actually think out the effect on our perception of different motions of time, how they would affect our values, ideas of cause and effect, and so on. It may sound theoretical. After some time it ceases to be theoretical and can become very emotional. One's attitude to many things may begin to change from it.

JANUARY 20, 1950 It is strange how the idea of reversed time and different kinds of time is beginning to turn up in the most unexpected places. As though knowledge of time were the special way through which this age can come to esoteric ideas. Certainly the world is stuffed with inventions which make possible quite different impressions and observations of time from those ordinarily available in other ages, if people only stop to think what it is all about. Quite a good name for us all would be 'Time Exploration Company, Unlimited', don't you think?

MAY 1, 1950 The idea of reversed time is very interesting. For me one of the most striking things about it is the way it shows the actual working mechanism of certain principles of human conduct, which usually we only guess at in a vaguely ethical or philosophical way. And it shows why it is imperative to review all the relationships of our life, and put understanding and right attitude *back into them now*, while we are still alive. For in this way only could we really affect that unrolling of time. To put understanding back into the past—this seems the practical possibility to which the idea points.

MARCH 22, 1951 I know that there is a part in us which, if we can find it and appeal through it, can know and do the impossible. The logical mind does not know these secrets and cannot know them. But there is a place hidden in the heart which does know and can tell us. Only one has to listen very deeply to hear it, and after it has spoken one must not let logical mind explain it away or tell us that it is unpractical or imagination. I have known people lose very big understanding that was given them, by explaining it away afterwards as imagination.

Later, one will find that all the things one understands or that are required of one in this way do accord with the laws and knowledge that were given to us. Only one must not expect them to tally with *our interpretation* of those laws. On the contrary, such new understanding will reveal laws in a completely new and unsuspected light.

For instance, all the literally miraculous things that happened at Ouspensky's death, and everything that has developed since —both for me personally and in relation to his work as a whole —convince me that he did not die as ordinary men die, but that he reached a level where a man becomes immortal*, or at any rate where he is not confined to time as we know it, but can act and make connections through time. I would have come to this conclusion through my personal experience. But I find that of all the extraordinary, miraculous and even fantastic things that happened and continue to happen, there is not one the possibility of which he did not explain to us in full detail while he was alive.

Further, if he did so become independent of time, or if he acquired fourth body* (if you like to be technical), then he is accessible now to anyone who desires his help with sufficient urgency and belief.

The lectures, the whole system as he explained it, was indeed the explanation of how to do the impossible, of how miracles are achieved. How then should we be surprised that Ouspensky himself actually put this knowledge to the use for which it was intended, and evidently expected those who followed him to take it in the same way? Looking back, I am appalled to remember how we took it all as a method of making slight adjustments to our personal psychology, and even judged the ultimate possibilities and him too on this level.

The ideas he explained do refer to the objective world, and if we think about them and work on them, we do prepare to orientate ourselves in that world when we get there. They are a very accurate map of that place. But to get there, we must go *through ourselves* and get out the other side.

'Believe in the impossible, for then you will find it possible.' Make yourself quiet, ask your heart what you are to believe and do, then cling to that and do it with all the force you can muster. And never let the voice of logic and probability prevent you.

JUNE 1, 1951 The question of actual contact with Ouspensky

—through time or however it is—seems to be the key question, and no longer for a few lucky individuals but on a larger scale. We need to think much about the possibility of change through right appeal to higher powers or higher man, the conditions under which this can be done, and the laws to which such appeal and contact would be subject.

May 1, 1952 The idea of different times is extremely illusive, and probably has to be so, because if it becomes logical and obvious it means that it has already degenerated to the level of our ordinary mind and ordinary perception of time. For me, the key to the understanding of this idea up to a certain point lies in Ouspensky's theory of six dimensions[1]—the first, second and third are clearly the length, breadth and thickness of space; the fourth is the line of time that we recognise, the line of individual life; the fifth is infinite repetition of this life and all it contains—the 'eternal now'; the sixth must be the dimension in which all exists everywhere, all possibilities are realised, and all is one. The fourth dimension is 'time', the fifth 'eternity', but what shall we call the sixth? For us it is Divinity itself.

Many philosophies have failed because they tried to jump directly from the fourth to the sixth without taking into account the strange overawing nature of the fifth dimension. On the other hand, to study the fifth—eternal recurrence—without taking into account the glorious possibilities of the sixth means to lose oneself in a blind alley of pessimism. We must search unremittingly for a crack through which we can pass to the sixth, or through which the sixth can enter directly into us.

May 20, 1952 Some time ago it seemed to me that each 'new renaissance' produced by school is based not only on the whole body of esoteric knowledge but specially on a new understanding of one particular part of it. For example, all sides of the Italian Renaissance seem to have been coloured by a new attitude towards three-dimensional space and its laws, the basic principles of which were formulated by Pacioli in *The Divine Proportion*. Even geographically, with the discovery of Amer-

[1] See note on Dimensions for R's later correction of this idea. J. C. S.

ica and the Indies, space changed and the world was revealed as having a different and immensely greater shape. Astronomical space too was revealed in a new and more complete way by the studies which sprang from this first key idea. For example, Kepler's proof of the true shape of the solar system was a direct result of his study of the Platonic solids and Pacioli's interpretation of them. The development in nearly all fields up to the middle of the nineteenth century seemed elaborations of the same line.

All this particularly interests me in relation to the question, What comparable key have we been given at this moment of renaissance in our tradition? The more I think about it the more it seems to me that our key, given to us by Ouspensky, is the idea of the three dimensions of time, and the period of shifting dimensions* for different cosmoses. It seems to me that this key has the possibilities of resolving all the problems of our age and connecting them with the central idea of man's development and his relation to the universe, in exactly the same way as Pacioli's ideas about space and the divine proportion contained the possibility of resolving all the problems of his time and relating them to this central idea.

Everywhere you look, experts seem to have reached the point of the idea of six dimensions with all its implications, and this idea alone can crystallise out the solution.

December 12, 1952 No one felt the tragedy of Russia more acutely than Ouspensky. But he knew or found something else. He knew and proved that while on one line of time—that to which the newspapers refer—everything decent, everything true is being and will be corrupted, both for our dying civilisation and for individuals, on another invisible line all possibilities actually exist, all can be remade and redeemed, both the past and future, personal and historical.

The joke is that those different dimensions of time, about which the mathematicians now begin to pose and solve questions like the ones about nuts and oranges in the algebra-books, have actual existence. And that while some are indeed filled with inevitable tragedy, corruption and crime, others contain very different lines of development indeed.

SEPTEMBER 20, 1954 The present moment is the point of escape from our three-dimensional prison of space and time. For in *this present moment*, remembering oneself, one can put oneself in contact with a place outside time, and with the help of eternity, where all possibilities in their fulness are already waiting. We must squeeze all its contents out of each moment.

HEART

NOVEMBER 5, 1949 The whole thing, the most difficult thing, is to wake the heart. Somehow one has to learn to be able to live in the heart, to judge from the heart, as ordinarily we live in mechanical mind and judge from that. It is shifting the centre of attention in oneself. For the movements of the heart are so quick that only if one can learn to live there for some time, is it possible to catch them as they pass and obey them. This also means that we have to learn to feed the heart, taking emotional impressions directly there; just as we now take knowledge directly into the mind.

There are methods to help in this. Ouspensky said: 'Make great demands upon yourself.' This is the key. Only they must be not only demands of fakir*, but demands of all kinds —particularly emotional demands. And all this must always be *combined with the effort for self-remembering**—and never become separated from that.

AUGUST 29, 1951 If only we had 'purified emotional centre' many things would become so much easier for us. Really it *is* pure—only other voices take it up so quickly that we don't distinguish what is said. If one learns to listen to heart, it will tell one things so clearly—what must be done, what must *not* be done, the real nature of people and places and things. Only it speaks so quietly, so subtly, and immediately a flood of reactions, explanations, excuses, theories have swamped it, and we do not even recognise it speak. Only *listening* carefully to what it wants to say, and remaining still until it has spoken, one cannot really do the wrong thing.

MARCH 6, 1952 Esoteric relationships have to be human relationships transmuted to something higher. They can never be less than human relationships.

MARCH 5, 1952 The heart understands all languages. The gift of tongues already fell on it, if we only knew. So we have to communicate from the heart, then the rest can take care of itself.

APRIL 27, 1952 The friendship of those in esoteric work must be a human one, but I feel that if it is only a human one—however understanding—it is doomed to degenerate. Really we can only love each other for any length of time in relation to what we are going to become and to what we serve. As we are and without common allegiance to the highest, however many different forms that may take, we can neither give nor merit lasting love. And I think it is quite right that we can't. For if there could be lasting love between us as we are, this would be an almost impassable barrier on the way to change.

AUGUST 27, 1952 This is the whole thing—to listen to the voice of the heart.

SEPTEMBER 9, 1952 There is often civil war within us that can only be resolved by doing what we have to do, by following the dictates of our heart. We must all, happy or unhappy, lonely or loved, come to that. There is no other way. It means seeing the nature of God in all that reaches us. Those who begin to see that are together, no matter where they are.

SEPTEMBER 12, 1952 Sometimes, when people asked Ouspensky about self-remembering, he said: 'Bring heart to head.' I think there is another movement which we also have to learn, especially when alone—bringing head to heart. Balance between two modes of perception depends on it. Sometimes there is too much pressure in one place, sometimes in the other. Harmonised, they can hardly make mistakes.

SEPTEMBER 3, 1954 We have to recognise Truth, however it speaks to us, whether with the voice of another or in our own hearts.

OCTOBER 26, 1954 To find truth, head and heart must work together in the right way. So often, head and heart have the bad habit of cancelling each other out. Heart understands something, but later in a different mood, head explains it away. Then heart becomes discouraged, loses faith in itself, and falls into melancholy.

I believe we must learn to perceive much more sensitively and constantly with the heart. But this is only possible if it receives the full support of head. Mind must bring reason and principles and tradition to justify and fix into permanent understanding the heart's fleeting glimpses of conscience and certainty.

There is hardly a person in our work who has not had his own glimpses of the miraculous, who has not at one time or another *known* his true connection with higher worlds. But our problem is fickleness. By talking in a doubting or cynical way about their own deepest feelings, by trying to make these feelings too reasonable and acceptable to others who have not shared them, people dissolve their own certainty. Then later they do not know what they know. To fix understanding it is necessary to affirm, affirm and affirm. Affirmation is the right attitude of the mind to the heart, of reason to conscience.

In a big way, I think the future of the whole Work turns on the same point. Everybody has at one time or another known inner direction from a higher level. If two or three hundred people in the whole Work, or even fifty, *permanently* lived under this direction and carried it out, there is no limit to what could be achieved. The great plan of Higher School*, of which Gurdjieff, Ouspensky and Nicoll are agents, would begin to be realised in this world on a completely different scale.

When I saw Dr Nicoll in 1952, he said that this time made one think of that before the coming of Christ. I was startled, because it corresponds so exactly with my own feeling. Now I realise that he spoke from very great understanding. There is an enormous work of preparation to be done in a very short time. We have to create a field of harmony into which some unimaginable great experiment can be launched. It means harmonising all branches of human knowledge, all types and divisions of men, all religions and philosophies. Not standardising them, but harmonising them—that is helping each to find itself, its true role.

PRAYER

September 29, 1950 There are certain principles even about prayer. Ouspensky always used to say, 'I cannot argue with preconceived ideas.' If one went to him, asking, 'This is what I have decided to do. Is it all right?', he would just say, 'Well . . .' But if one went, saying: 'The situation is like this. What can I do?' then he would always have some new light to throw on it, which revealed some quite unexpected course. I think it is the same with prayer. Maybe, for example, someone prays to God to take away desire. But supposing desire is exactly what he needs, only so strong that it breaks through into a different realm altogether? He says to God: 'This is what I decided, please help me attain it.' But supposing he saw the whole thing from the wrong point of view, and his request was based on this wrong point of view—what can happen to such a prayer?

I think prayer, or some appeal from the whole heart to a force outside our circle of life which alone can alter things there, is the only possibility in certain insoluble circumstances. But surely we must cry to be shown the way out, to be shown the unseen ladder out of the impasse, and be very ready to accept *whatever* is shown. Then if some new idea, some new light comes into one's heart—as it will—one must be prepared to obey courageously. If one does so, one will be led out of the maze.

One must first take full responsibility for one's past; and having done so, realise that only with higher help can one's future change. Then something may be possible.

July 22, 1952 For us it is established without doubt that all sincere appeal for help *must* receive an answer. But it's form is always unexpected.

February 13, 1953 Surely the *attempt* to 'bridge the gap between the world of everyday fact and the world of great laws' is the key to all progress, to the possibility of getting help, to the possibility of disillusion, revelation or what you will. Every saint and scientist worth his salt started in this way, and unless one does so start, my experience—confirmed more strongly every year—is that nothing good happens or can happen.

JANUARY 11, 1956 Some situations *cannot* be resolved by men alone. We need a miracle to resolve them and we have every right to pray for a miracle. It is not a bad sign that things get darker before they get lighter.

MARCH 5, 1956 The miraculous happens to people and they feel it, but they can't quite believe it because all its justifications in print belong to an age which they call superstitious. Feeling the miraculous is something to do with getting one's eye in. We are so used to physical explanations that if a figure of light should appear before us, we would say it was something wrong with the television.

MARCH 11, 1956 Hope and faith are our greatest weapons. As long as we have them, everything is possible. With hope and faith we *demand* to be on another level—and it will never be denied us.

HIGHER STATES

July 31, 1948 It seems clear that we cannot command the working of higher centres*, but that with right preparation of the different faculties, even a slight working of these centres may yield very great understanding indeed, whereas without preparation the same functioning of higher centres would give no more than a temporary sense of exultation or freedom. It is evidently not only a question of degree of consciousness but what that degree is made to yield, so to speak. This is very variable indeed. And one begins to see the point of Ouspensky's very great stress on *understanding* as the key of our way—with understanding the same effort, the same degree of consciousness, may yield ten times the result as without.

June 20, 1951 In higher states gratitude changes into something else. It changes into knowledge of what one has to do, and even—if it is intense enough—into power to carry that out.

November 6, 1951 Sometimes it seems appallingly tedious to have to write something out at full length, page after page after page, for someone to read page after page after page in the same way, when its whole point lies in one simultaneous perception. Painting begins to seem much more interesting to me. Certainly it has to be painted stroke after stroke after stroke, but it is seen *all at once*, in one blow. That begins to seem to me like a better simulation of higher centres. Only perhaps we have to perform the compression internally first. I think the most heavenly ecstasy would be to know *at once* five hundred things which we have already known very well separately.

November 14, 1951 Telepathy—and the theory of telepathy—interests me very much. I think it must be studied in two aspects. As in radio or television, there is first the carrier-wave, second the message to be conveyed. For telepathy, I think the carrier-wave is something of the nature of highest emotional energy, which has to be generated in tremendous intensity—perhaps by fasting, suffering, endurance—in order to make transmission possible. But supposing transmission is achieved, what message would be sent? This is work for ordinary mind and understanding, and I believe can be practised for all the time. If you go through all your friends one by one, say for five minutes each, and recreate your relationship with them as it now stands, almost certainly there will arise in your mind some message you would wish to send—something you wish to explain, to ask forgiveness for, to tell. Then if so, you can practise holding in your mind the image of this person, your relationship to them, combined with the message and only with the message you wish to send. To me this is practical preparation for telepathy, possible in our state.

The other question is to make ourselves sensitive to the *reception* of telepathy, able to distinguish and preserve ideas and messages which enter our minds from a higher level. I believe this in fact happens much more often than we think, but that such ideas and messages are ordinarily sucked into the flood of our own personal thought and thus very soon lose their nature and power. We have to learn to recognise the *reception* of higher ideas in the moment it occurs. This can lead to many other things.

FEBRUARY 18, 1952 There are questions very difficult to express logically, and explanations which seem logically contradictory, which may be only imperfect ways of trying to describe different aspects which in a higher state are seen as *one*, as a single whole. In a higher state, different possibilities may not appear mutually exclusive, as they do in our time, but may be seen to exist together. Only when we discuss it all logically, with our view of time, difficulties arise.

JUNE 16, 1952 The study of types* is both fascinating and elusive. The more material one gathers about them, the more one feels that some key to their understanding is missing. And in the end one comes to feel that this missing key is in fact connected with our ordinary state. Types can only really be recognised and classified from a different level of consciousness.

AUGUST 15, 1952 I think it is impossible for a man to get to higher states by his own efforts alone—some higher power must come down from above to help him. Only lightning can produce certain results. But man must make his own conductor and thrust it high above the surrounding jungle in order to attract the lightning. Even then he may have to wait a long time before it strikes. But when it does then its power, not his, will show him everything.

The same idea is put in another way, with very exact indications, in the table in *In Search of the Miraculous*, which shows what all creatures eat and are eaten by. Only, just as a potato, if raw is eaten by pigs, if cooked by men, and if rotten by worms, so the essence of man may be eaten by different powers, according to what he himself has made of it. And if he can get himself eaten by Divinity, this would indeed be help from above—the lightning stroke.

SEPTEMBER 24, 1952 People who have had experiences must begin to be able to judge them objectively and assess their value and their danger themselves. In the chapter called 'Experimental Mysticism' in *A New Model*, one can see how Ouspensky carried the weapon of self-remembering into new states and unknown worlds. The stranger it all is, the more scrupulous must one be to question everything and to purge it all of one's old self. Most important of all, when one comes back, one must never allow oneself to use one's experiences as a club with which to beat others. For in this way the experiences themselves are corrupted, and all is lost.

DECEMBER 11, 1952 Sometimes one finds oneself in surroundings one knows—the sights and scenes and people are all just the same as always, but suddenly something from a different world seems to show through them. Each detail is not only familiar in itself, but all at once a symbol of something else much more important as well. Perhaps really the world is always like this but only occasionally we see it so.

SEPTEMBER 7, 1953 Telepathy, when it really exists, can be either accidental, or conscious and meaningful. Conscious telepathy needs much understanding, great power of attention and special technique. It does not 'happen'.

OCTOBER 21, 1953 There is a hint about 'growing down' in the idea that each faster function*, made conscious, gives access to one larger cosmos and one smaller one. Thus the ordinary mental function gives access to the world of man. The instinctive function connects above with the world of Nature and below with the world of cells. The emotional function connects above with the world of Earth and below with the world of molecules. The higher mental function connects above with the Solar World and below with the world of electrons. I know this is very theoretical but if one considers it deeply and connects it with one's own experiences, it seems to throw quite a lot of light on many things that Jung found or guessed.

BODY, SOUL AND SPIRIT

DECEMBER 31, 1951 I think every living cosmos—whether planet or civilisation or man or school—must have spirit, soul and body, must live in three worlds and three vehicles simultaneously, since this is the great universal pattern. And that school* must externally create form, organisation and monuments—even though these are not the essential. For without them it cannot really touch this world, in which we and all men live after all.

NOVEMBER 14, 1952 All men have the birthright of a soul in embryo. But this embryo must in some way be fertilised to start the process by which it can become conscious and develop its full stature.

I myself connect this 'fertilisation' of the soul with school. But this is a very big word and the fertilising influence of school may take many forms, as did Zeus in the Greek myths. Nearly always, I think, it must manifest through a living man or woman, one's master or something like that. But now I would not like to rule out other possibilities—though if they exist the principle must be the same.

I suppose it can be said that one can hasten the growth of conscious soul. Yet sometimes I wonder if that is putting it quite right. Can we do anything but what we are impelled by our own inner hunger and need to do? And again, at what stages is it necessary to be active, and at what stages passive? It all remains very mysterious really. We must remember that.

SEPTEMBER 6, 1954 Our work is to realise conscious harmony. First in oneself individually. Then in one's group. Then gradually between groups and so projected infinitely out into the world. Individually, we must realise harmony between all our functions, all our interests, all our duties, all sides of our life—dedicating the harmonious whole to God and to the Work. This is what our studies are preparing us for. They have no other purpose.

Each person has to recreate the whole System intellectually for himself and in himself. This is the scaffolding of his new creation. Nobody else can do it for him, and what he finds is his own.

At the same time, the construction of one's own intellectual 'model of the universe' is *only* scaffolding. This is the skeleton. A new kind of living flesh must grow upon it, a new body. What does this mean? It means learning to live in the soul and from the soul.

When one does this, all the complicated structure of ideas which one has created resolves into something very simple, very direct.

What is our work all about? It is to enable man to live consciously in three bodies, in three worlds, and so realise the Divine Plan. A physical body was given him by Nature at birth. Somewhere exists the original Divine spark launched from God and which, refound, will be his conscious spirit. But ordinary man has no feeling for that body which was created to connect the two—the soul.

The soul is the bridge between body and spirit, between earth and Heaven. It is there, but you have to become aware of it, you have to feel it, you have to live in it.

You feel the soul by opening your heart to people, by accepting what is. The soul grows through the heart. The heart is the door of the soul. But with all ordinary man, this door is blocked with fear, prejudice, doubt. His heart is not open to the world. He only takes from it what he wants to take, in the way he wants to take it. If he could just *be himself*, *be his whole self*, without fear and without self-protection, he would already live from the soul. So learn simply to *be*, to *be* your *whole* self.

First you must live in awareness of your physical body. Then in awareness of your soul. Then in awareness of your spirit.

There is one thing more. Everyone who goes far in this Work must learn how to rest. The tensions which he meets will be too strong for him otherwise. In fact there is only one true kind of rest—this is in the thought of God, in the remembrance of God, in God.

There are two visions of the Universe. And we have to learn to cultivate them alternately. One is the vision of the Hierarchy of Beings, of the ladder up which we and all others must struggle by labour, sacrifice, service, understanding. This is the way of School. The other is the direct vision of God, of a Divine vibration which pervades and sustains all beings everywhere, from rock to Christ, from moon to sun. These two visions are the day and the night of our work. We labour in the one, we rest in the other. It has to be like that.

This is why our Tradition is not a substitute for religion. It is the complement of it. Every man needs a religion, and probably a Church, to sustain him in the vision of God.

FEBRUARY 23, 1955 The whole thing lies in the relation of body, soul and spirit. Body vibrates—more in some than in others, but it vibrates. Spirit vibrates—somewhere. But the soul is very inert, it usually quivers only on the surface, not deeply. We have to make it vibrate throughout, right to its deepest part. It is shaken by joy, pain, loss, discovery, hard decisions, payment, all kind of things. By self-remembering this vibration is carried deep, the whole soul vibrates with it. When the whole soul vibrates as strongly as the body and spirit, then the three vibrate as one. We are one. We are real. We have integrity.

So really we have to be grateful for soul-shaking, though God knows it may be uncomfortable enough at the time. Perhaps our mistake is that we want peace in the wrong place. People ask for peace in their souls—they should ask for turmoil in their souls, so that they may find real peace in their spirits.

Conscience is the voice of the spirit penetrating through the soul to the body, when the three are vibrating together. Self-remembering brings this about—body, soul and spirit are momentarily aligned. The body is connected through the soul to the spirit, which is outside time, immortal. That is why in moments of self-remembering there is no time, nor fear, nor doubt—only pure consciousness, silence, and the voice of conscience. Lose self-remembering, and time, fear and doubt immediately return.

A lot of the austerity and suffering which the System*

entailed in the old days was because Ouspensky staked everything on the spirit. He would accept no rewards in the world of the soul, either for himself or his people. He staked all the winnings on spirit, and won. He became free spirit. Then everything changed. Because if we wish we can now allow his spirit to act on our souls, make them alive, make them vibrate. Then through this vivification of our souls, by self-remembering, we can feel our own spirits. In them is absolute certainty, security and truth.

MARCH 14, 1955 We all have good qualities and we all have repulsive features. On the level of qualities, good or bad, nothing can be done. But we have a spirit which is immortal, and all our efforts at self-remembering are to make a conscious connection with it. One can think of the body as a beautiful and marvellously ingenious instrument—or as an old bag of bones, whichever one likes. In either case it only has meaning if it serves the spirit, through the intermediary of the conscious soul which we are trying to make.

So we must look up, lift our longing, try always to feel up, in space. When we get that sensation we will never lose it. And all that is repulsive will remain below us.

SEPTEMBER 28, 1955 Reach the invisible by the visible—the spiritual by the physical. The soul is the bridge. But can you distinguish between those three worlds, those three qualities? When you have established contact with the spiritual you will have confidence in that which has to be done.

NOVEMBER 15, 1955 The soul is the bridge, the connection, between body and spirit. Those who live wholly from the bodies' impulses and vanities—you can say that they have no soul, or that their soul is asleep; you feel it. Those who live groping for the truth, trying to obey conscience—their souls are growing, their souls are waking; you feel that too. Really everyone has a soul, but one has to become aware of it, live in it, make it vibrate. When it really vibrates, the connection between body and spirit is completed. What makes the soul vibrate, and so allows the whole man to act as one? Struggle, faith, effort, will, pain and joy and memory and compassion and sacrifice. All these belong to the coming alive of the soul.

We recognise the spirit by *conscience*, which is its voice; we recognise the body by taking *thought* for it; we recognise the soul by *will*—will by which man makes his body obey his spirit, and so unifies himself. The body has its emanations and the spirit has its emanations. Each effort of will, by which a man makes his physical action accord with his conscience, fuses an atom of body with an atom of spirit to form a molecule of soul. And just as atoms of hydrogen and atoms of oxygen can exist side by side for ever without forming water till fused by the shock of electrolysis, so spirit and body can exist indefinitely side by side till the shock of will makes of their fusion the new substance soul.

The body lives in space and time, subject to matter, illusion and sense. The spirit lives in eternity and truth. The soul must unite the two. So all that is certainty belongs to the spirit, all that is struggle belongs to the soul. The spirit knows God, the soul has faith; the spirit knows God, the soul has hope; the spirit knows God, the soul has charity. This is how the soul is made to vibrate, and man becomes one, becomes himself.

TRACES OF SCHOOL

MARCH 23, 1952 The subject of the Rome school is very interesting. My feeling is that as time goes on, those who study this line will find that more and more of the vital influences of the nineteenth century derive from that source.

SEPTEMBER 16, 1952 It was most interesting while in Florence to find how every creative line, every skill and understanding of the Renaissance, can be traced back to the actual Medici household—to one particular group in one place. And also interesting that the whole thing—the bringing of scholars from the East, the backing of Donatello, Michael Angelo, Fra Angelico, the building of churches, collecting of libraries, foundation of the Platonic Academy—was all paid for and made possible by the Medici banking business. For those who are interested in the role of business in relation to esoteric influence, there's the classic example.

JANUARY 22, 1953 Fabre d'Olivet's cosmology is curiously reminiscent of some of the ancient American sacred books, like the Popol Vuh and the Chilan Balam. After magnificent cosmological beginnings like the Book of Genesis, they turn into bloodthirsty epics about races of giants and dwarfs who eat each other, cut each other in pieces and bury each other alive—all rather terrifying until one realises that they are talking about geological processes and epochs.

APRIL 4, 1954 I see our way as the great harmoniser of all previous esoteric experiments, as it is of all sides of human nature. Now everything must be brought together into consciousness, nothing left out. A supreme effort is being made to reconcile what before had to be divided. Understanding, love, will, unified by consciousness, make it possible.

MARCH 2, 1954 Of all the Oriental ways, Zen Buddhism seems nearest to Western mentality and outlook. But personally, with every year I live on this continent, I become more convinced that the Oriental ways are not for us. Here in Latin America particularly, those who dabble in them seem to get into a backwater, cut off from all that is real and living in this time and this place. I am sure that a new complete way is being created for the West, and that before the Oriental traditions can be absorbed into this way they have to go through a deep transformation.

Now one begins to realise the tremendous scale on which Ouspensky was seeing, when, after abandoning the System*, he said: 'You must reconstruct everything. Everything must be remade from the very beginning.' It now seems to me that this reconstruction is something which is being launched from Great School*, and that it is connected with a crossroads in the history of humanity as important as that represented by the coming of Christ.

It was always said about the Fourth Way* that it had to be followed *in life*, and that it consisted in developing consciousness simultaneously in all centres*. Yet all that has been known about the Fourth Way till now seems only a prelude to the way which is now gradually being revealed by Great School to the West. For this new way seems to be based on the science of conscious harmony. It means creating harmony between all man's functions, and between all sides of his life. It means creating harmony between the different types* in a group. It means creating harmony between all the traditional ways—and beyond that, on another scale, between peoples, races and ages.

Somehow, compared with this complete vision, the traditional Yoga and monastic ways, which leave out or amputate so many sides and triumphs of modern life, seem out of date and artificial. I know now that we have been shown the beginning of this new way, and that the more we realise what we have been given, the more will be revealed to us. The new way couldn't come fully fledged into the world, because it is based on understanding, and understanding must grow.

But it is being released at a tremendous speed and through many different channels simultaneously. One has to learn to put the pieces of the jigsaw puzzle together. And this depends on being able to put one's own inner jigsaw puzzle together—all of it, without leaving any pieces out.

Even so, perhaps all that we can now bring to realisation of this new way is but preparing the ground for a great demonstration which will be made from above at the critical moment. Somehow many seem to recognise this and focus their eyes past the apparently insoluble present, to some tremendous and miraculous hope in the future.

OCTOBER 4, 1954 I believe that all the moments of rebirth in history have the same quality and stem from the same truth. It is only in their degeneration that ideas seem irreconcilable.

NOVEMBER 3, 1954 In Rome we found very many clues about the nameless nineteenth-century circle which launched so many creative currents into European life. It was founded by Cagliostro just before his imprisonment in 1789. Goethe was strongly affected by it though at a distance. Among the French who belonged to it in the first thirty years were Ingres, Chateaubriand, Ampère père et fils, Champollion, Madame Recamier. Among the Germans, Baron Bunsen the chemist, who devoted his life to understanding between the Catholic and Protestant churches, Mendelssohn, the painters Cornelius, Shadow and Overbeck, the historian Niebuhr. Among the Russians, the painters Kiprensky and Ivanov, Gogol the writer, and Stukovsky who became tutor to Alexander the Second. Among others the Danish sculptor Thorwaldsen, the Hungarian musician Liszt, the English poet Shelley, the Danish archaeologist Zoega and the Italian composer Rossini. In a later generation came Browning, Ibsen, Nietsche, Stevenson and many, many others.

Their centre was round the Via Gregoriana and Via Sistina. For a long time they worked in the French Academy at the Villa Medici. They restored the churches of Santa Trinidad dei Monte and San Andrea delle Fratte. Ingres formed a parallel group in Paris, which developed on its own, independent yet connected. These groups were, I believe, the real inspiration of the nineteenth-century culture.

We were also looking at the early Christian churches of the third to fifth centuries, when such an effort was made to reconcile the ancient Graeco-Egyptian wisdom with the new Christian revelation.

DECEMBER 10, 1954 It is fascinating when we see patterns, traditional patterns in which we at the moment happen to figure, but which were there long before us, and will go on repeating long after us. More and more the repository of all patterns seems to be the Gospel Drama. If one understands the way different types and levels reacted then, one will recognise those reactions always and everywhere.

Why does the story of the disciples going to Emmaus seem the original performance of our work? Perhaps the two disciples were really disillusioned after the Crucifixion, they were going away because they thought it was all over. But as they went out into the world, Christ appeared to them. Even then they did not recognise, until they invited Him to stay for a meal and a drink. Then their eyes were opened. It was their worldly kindness and hospitality which woke them and revealed Him. When they awoke and recognised, then they had to rush back to try to wake the official disciples at headquarters, who were busy making a policy out of their own uncertainty. Of course they were not believed. But as soon as those who had gone and those who stayed were together again, Christ appeared to them all, welded them into the new beginning.

I think the way to Emmaus is the Fourth Way. In the Fourth Way people have to be disillusioned at home, to go out bravely into the world to find truth, to be illumined *there*, and then bring light home again.

DECEMBER 29, 1954 I wonder why the Sufi experiment managed to hit such a pure ecstatic note? It seems to me that something went very right, and at a certain point negative emotions were transmitted into love on a very big scale.

In *The Whirling Ecstasy** there is a place where Jellaledin sends his son to look for Shems, saying: 'If you find him, throw 2000 gold ashrafi under the feet of the Sultan of Tabriz.' When will we understand this attitude? When will we see that this is the royal road to freedom?

MARCH 21, 1955 There is still much to be found in the Middle East—Syria, Egypt, Palestine and Persia—the traces of many early experiments of the Fourth Way. I believe all these clues have to be gathered together while there is still time, to be incorporated in this great culminating demonstration of the Fourth Way which belongs to our time.

JULY 20, 1955 Last year we went looking for the traces of schools in the past—Early Christian schools in Rome, Gothic cathedral schools in France, and that nineteenth-century school in Rome again, from which came *Peer Gynt* and so many other wonderful things. We did find a lot, and in a way difficult to describe, one seems also to make a living connection through time back to those experiments.

Later we began to see how the study of past schools draws one more and more strongly towards that greatest and most perfect demonstration of school on earth, the Gospel Drama and the Passion of Christ. One sees that that is the focus and example of all school work in all ages, and that every experiment is an attempt to reflect it in one way or another.

Although we didn't fully understand this when we started, it is now clear that this last trip was a journey in search of the Passion. In Holy Week in Seville we saw how men have tried to re-live it for themselves. In the Egyptian temples and on the Greek islands we saw how for thousands of years schools were preparing men to understand what was to come. In Jerusalem, of course, we saw the actual scenery and the soil against which the Drama was played, and one was made to visualise in a very vivid way the struggles and hopes and betrayals and liberation of those actual men and women. In Jerusalem, too, one sees everything that men make of higher influence—it is a complete world, full of inspiration, superstition, cruelty, fear and faith.

Then we moved on to the Eastern countries, into the Moslem world, to Damascus, Baghdad, Teheran and Isfahan. I was quite unprepared for the sensation that the very air changes when you leave the Christian world. Something is missing which we take so much for granted that we don't even think of it. It is something to do with individual hope, recognition of the value of each individual soul. In the East, of course, there are wise men and good men and religious men, but I have never felt in the West this strange apathy and hopelessness among poor people, as though they have nothing to expect but death. Evidently the coming of Christ changed the whole nature and possibility of all levels of beings on the earth. Where this is not recognised, there is a curious stagnation. From this I understood in a new way what the 'conversion' of a country meant to the Apostles or to medieval missionaries. However imperfectly it might be done from a human point of view it meant an actual transmutation of human possibilities in that area. It was really a miraculous process.

Visiting dervishes and sufis in Egypt, Syria and Lebanon, we felt that their work was to bring in a kind of disguised Christianity where a country was not ready to accept it openly. Perhaps their role was to try to redeem some mistake Mohamet made.

Flying so quickly from country to country, and from one ancient site to another, one began to see history as a tremendous play of school influence, building, teaching, creating, disappearing from one place and appearing in another. One saw that school influence is life; where it is, there is hope and creation; where it disappears follows hopelessness and corruption. We also saw that the whole work of schools in the ancient world was to lead up to the coming of Christ, and the whole work of schools since has been to reveal what Christ actually brought.

This is our work also, in fact it is the only Work. But it is so big, so strange, and so many-sided that we had to come to it through a teaching where the name of Christ was hardly mentioned, lest it be taken on too low a level.

Evidently our work will be measured, not by what we say or write, but by the degree in which we can manifest charity. When it is present, there is happiness, understanding and harmony. When vanity and sleep take its place, everything becomes confused again. If things go wrong, as they certainly do, one knows that it is because one has failed to project conscious harmony. In so far as things go right, one realises that one has been helped to do so.

AUGUST 6, 1955 The whole thing is that people should search, search, search; try to be sincere; not imitate each other, me, Ouspensky, or anyone else; and respect the truth everywhere. The ones who won't imitate are much harder to handle, but infinitely more rewarding. In fact, they are the people we are looking for. Higher men* are those who have become completely original, unlike anyone else in the universe. Who have found their own way of being completely themselves, offering their whole selves to the Work, and accepting the consequences. It is not comfortable, because there are no precedents. As there were no precedents for an Ouspensky or a Gurdjieff.

I want people to study—study something, almost anything, deeply, from all angles; try to do original research, using what we have been given as the key of understanding. The system is too big to waste indefinitely on classifying the uninteresting contents of one's own mind. That's all right for a while. But then it must be used to project understanding into bigger fields.

Visiting those ancient sites—Karnak, Jerusalem, Damascus, Isfahan—one felt what tremendous concentration of knowledge they contain. Those places have such pressure of knowledge—more pounds per square inch than anywhere else. That is what attracts the tourists, though they do not know why. And we, who see ourselves in that company, are so ignorant, so uneducated. We haven't understood that being familiar with principles is one thing, harnessing knowledge to them is quite different. It is so important, in our time, that all knowledge be related to these principles and put safely in its place, not left loose and inflammable. For that is the way of disaster.

Skipping so quickly from one country to another—from Italy to Egypt, Jordan, Syria, Lebanon, Iraq, Persia, Turkey, Greece—one felt that all the human history which lies there so richly, like a deep fertile soil, is history of schools and school influence. The coming of school, its growth in one place, its transfer elsewhere, the spread of the temples, philosophies, arts and symbols which it leaves behind, the golden ages of its triumph, the great figures which represent it, the destruction which comes at the end of its cycle, the corruption which follows its betrayal—this is human history, there isn't anything else. And we have to collect all that, make it feed the present.

All through the trip the feeling grew that the drama of Christ is the centre of human history. Earlier and later times flow out from there like ripples from a splash. There is only one hierarchy*, one Inner Circle. Before Christ they were preparing men to understand what He was going to bring; since, they have been preparing man to understand what He already brought. But it's all the same work.

At the time of Christ a tremendous break was made: it was something like reversing the current. Everything that had gone before had to appear wrong and evil. But now, as part of today's work of harmony, we have to re-understand the ancient world and its mysteries, show that it all belongs to the same work, all points in the same direction.

I think that if people could understand that there always had been one and the same Hierarchy guiding man, that Hercules and Buddha and Solomon, the disciples who physically surrounded Christ, and still others who have created the modern world in which we live were all part of it, then many things would be much clearer and simpler for them. They would understand that fanaticism, fear, contradiction and persecution is something ordinary men have introduced into all this. There cannot be contradiction in the original impulses of school, because they all came from the same place and were part of a single plan. But in order to understand this, people must study, work, investigate, experiment. Then they will prove it to themselves and to others.

OCTOBER 5, 1955 In Egypt, especially in Luxor, one saw all the wisdom of the ancient world locked up, waiting to be rediscovered. But one also saw that *then* the chances were only for a few, and that all *that* was but preparation for what Christ was going to bring. The Egyptians themselves knew it. In the Ptolemaic temples, 100 years before Christ, suddenly appears a chapel of the Nativity, the Mammesi. And there it all is, in Egyptian style, the Annunciation and everything else that was going to happen.

There is something parallel in Peru and Egypt—they have

the same root—perhaps Atlantis, and the same ancient wisdom. But Peru is rising, and Egypt falling. Is it because Peru is making the bridge between the ancient world and Christianity, and Egypt not? Or is it something to do with the unknown destiny of the New World?

February 10, 1956 We have been studying the history of culture and art as trace of School. We had one evening on the Egyptians, their gods, their architecture and their hieroglyphs. Then there was one about the Phoenicians and the Jews, about the dances, the meaning of the alphabet, and Solomon's Temple. Then about the Greeks, how they discovered freedom of individual conscience, and felt the laws of rhythm and harmony in everything they did. There was another about the situation in the first century before Christ, the corruption and prostitution of the old ways, and the intimation of something new to come. We talked about the profound contrast between the old ways, among a closed priesthood for selected initiates, who were taught in darkness and mystery, and who tried to make the form immortal with their mummies and tombs and temples, and Christ's teaching in the open air on the highroad to any who wished to hear in the daily circumstances of their lives. Strange that there are so many physical traces of Egypt, none at all of the first three centuries of Christianity—no tombs, no temples, no art. But a path had been opened in a completely different dimension. Art and physical symbolism only enter with the wise men from Alexandria, St. Clement, Origen, and the others who had been brought up in the old tradition.

DIFFERENT WAYS

APRIL 4, 1949 There are very big reasons indeed why different ways should not be mixed. Bacon and eggs are a beautiful invention, so is strawberry ice-cream, but mixed together they cease to be human food. It is the same on a higher level.

But the need to keep ways separate does not at all mean that people belonging to different ways may not meet, and become the best of friends, and individually learn from each other. If they fail to learn from each other, they are missing a very great opportunity indeed. But it only becomes possible if the fundamental principle is recognised, and ceases to be seen as personal.

About things in school* way that seem puzzling, I would only say that in school, things are not what they seem—and only after fifteen years I begin to learn that by judging one cannot understand.

NOVEMBER 4, 1950 More and more I feel that *inside* the Work the understanding of unity, and the gradual melting down of suspicions and resistances, is one of our most important tasks. It does not mean compromise or mixing. On the contrary, each group ought to be able to do their own work better with a larger understanding of the whole.

It seems to me that a new phase is being reached. In the two or three years after Ouspensky's death the chief work was to separate and consolidate his own friends, to introduce them to each other, help them to understand each other, make them one body in which the new level of understanding which Ouspensky made available could flow freely. If this separation had not been the chief emphasis all would have been swallowed up or scattered. But, under some kind of hidden direction, it has come about. There does exist a unity and understanding among Ouspensky's friends.

Now, I feel the emphasis shifts slightly. People must try to see things on a larger scale, try not to blame or judge or be afraid of other lines. If there were mistakes in our understanding of what we were given, somehow and sometime those mistakes have to be corrected, for our work as a whole to fulfil itself. And everything which makes for understanding and affection between different parts of our work makes that task easier; and everything which makes natural organic divisions into rigid impenetrable barriers makes it more difficult.

Certainly it is a slow patient work—and anything pressed too soon or in the wrong way will spoil rather than heal. But some time—in how many years we don't know—all sides of our work will join again; and we must always bear that in mind.

In my opinion the separation between Ouspensky and Gurdjieff had a very deep meaning—to enable different aspects of a big plan to develop without interfering with each other. And I feel the non-mixing of different lines still to be very important. The two lines of influence have a completely different *quality*—it is not that they should not but that they cannot mix. They are like oil and water.

The idea that individuals from the two lines should even meet is deeply shocking to some people. I do not mind such shakings. Things which shake us at the basis of our deepest loyalties, which make us weigh one good against another good, can purify beliefs and make people search deeper into themselves. This is all we can ask for.

JANUARY 3, 1951 I believe that all that has happened from the furthest back we can trace our ideas, right through to their widest effects in an unknown future, and including all the main characters concerned, is part of a very great and foreseen plan. I think Gurdjieff played a definite role in this pattern—partly in transmitting certain ideas from the East to the West, partly perhaps in giving Ouspensky something to struggle with worthy of his strength. If Gurdjieff himself had not played this role, then someone else would have had to play it.

I think the roles Ouspensky and Gurdjieff played in the very nature of the pattern involve struggle, apparent rivalry, conflicting aspects, or something like that—perhaps like those of Plato and Socrates, Jellaledin Rumi and Shemsedin. These two roles have to appear to clash in order for something greater still to be forged. 'Struggle without destruction.' To me this is sufficient to explain Ouspensky's parting from Gurdjieff, and the separation of their ways. I think this is inherent in the pattern of school-expression upon earth. It makes abundantly clear the necessity of not mixing. Those who try to mix these two poles understand neither the one nor the other.

But the boundaries between the two ways, although they must be clearly marked and preserved, must not be made impassable. If they are made impassable, this is not by the pattern, but by human rigidity and fear.

I believe that though the two ways cannot mix, understanding between them must be possible. I see with great vividness the train of misunderstandings, bitterness and calumny of the Work that must stretch into the future if an effort at understanding between them is not made. It even seems to me that in some distant time men might torture each other and even fight wars over it.

Again let me emphasise that I believe the Work to be one, though Ouspensky's and Gurdjieff's ways to be distinct and unmixable in themselves. But one thing I have learned in the last three years is that understandings and explanations, *apparently contradictory to our mind*, may be reconcilable on another level; because the whole is so immeasurably more complex and more wonderful than anyone can see.

MAY 1, 1952 According to my understanding, the 'system' that Ouspensky said he abandoned in the last stage of his life was the system developed in *In Search of the Miraculous*, or rather the language and manner of presentation, the exterior form of this system which had to be abandoned. The laws and principles that were indicated there cannot be abandoned, because they are laws of the universe itself. But what now becomes clear is that by one stroke he saved the system from becoming dogma to us, and our understanding from becoming frozen in words and set for us. At a certain point, with much work and attention, one must master a whole system of real knowledge. Then at another point one can advance further only by abandoning that system and continuing along the road without luggage. It seems contradictory, but it is so.

To my mind the most simple explanation of the separation of Ouspensky and Gurdjieff is that when he reaches a certain level of development a man has inevitably to separate from his teacher and create his own independent work and circle. It is his task to form his own sphere of influence. Then those who follow have to join either one teacher or the other, one sphere of influence or the other. They cannot belong to two, for the same reason that it is impossible for one cell to belong simultaneously to two bodies.

NOVEMBER 17, 1952 There is more than one system of philosophy which, although not directly in the same line as ours, seems to bear similarities in many respects. At the same time every man who rises above a certain level creates his own individual magnetic field which must not be mixed nor compared with that of another. Because it is his own and unique.

JANUARY 3, 1953 I am very impressed with the complementary nature of the groups in different countries. Each needs the others and their possibilities. Only in the sum of the different aspects of the Work in different parts of the world can one see the higher plan in its grandeur.

JULY 18, 1955 In my understanding the whole field of higher influences which was transmitted to us through Gurdjieff and Ouspensky forms a single whole, a world if you like. Those two strange and great men are the opposite poles of that world. That is why they had to separate. That is why, during their lives, one had to work with one or the other of them, just as one has to live either in the northern or southern hemisphere.

If one thinks of them as individuals they will always seem contradictory and antagonistic. If one thinks of what lies behind them, one will see that both they and their work were complementary, and that they were being used to launch into the world a great new esoteric experiment.

What is the final meaning of that experiment nobody knows yet. Perhaps it is to prepare the way for something that is yet to come. In any case it was to demonstrate the harmonious development of man, as Gurdjieff once called it.

SEPTEMBER 26, 1955 We can recognise those who are really *in* our work very quickly. For them the ideas are self-evident, they recognise that this is *different from anything else*. Those who are evidently new to our work have to argue and try to prove that it is just the same as what is said elsewhere. There are some people, perhaps very interested in philosophy or religion, who are not going our way at all and never will. They try to make everything that is given fit their own line—Buddhism, Andean politics, Yoga or whatever it may be.

DECEMBER 16, 1955 While it is good to find out everything one can about the work of different groups, it is better not to mix two lines of study.

RELIGION

NOVEMBER 12, 1951 I do not find religious language a difficulty. It has been suggested that in the process of transmitting the system from one generation to another, and one country to another, some ideas may have entered that should not have been there, and others that should have, were omitted. I think this is true, and one of the ideas which was (almost blasphemously) omitted was the idea of God. But then again perhaps it was omitted precisely in order that it should enter again later —in our time—as a new shock of immense force.

This connects in my mind with the question of the third force* in self-remembering*. For here also there seems to have been a quite intentional omission, since it was always explained in other connections that nothing can manifest except through the action of three forces, and that only two inevitably give no result. Yet the idea of third force in self-remembering seems never to have been spoken about, except in veiled hints at the end of Mr Ouspensky's life.

To me this idea is connected with our right relation with our teacher, with higher school*, with God, and thus with the whole plan of higher powers for the regeneration of mankind. The nature of the third force which makes self-remembering possible and miraculous, will appear different to different people according to their type. But to me the secret, the formula even, is contained in the phrase from St. John: 'Whatsoever ye shall ask of the Father in my name, he will give it to you.' It is Christ, every true esoteric teacher, our teacher, speaking. And I think it refers to the nature of the triad by which miracles are possible, and by which higher powers can act directly in our world.

APRIL 15, 1952 The Work could be described as work to make souls. But souls, once made, are still corruptible. If the work of Christ was to turn water into wine, that of the devil is to change wine into vinegar. It is said in this system, as in the esoteric tradition, that 'the devil eats souls'. Supposing that the work of schools is successful, and that the harvest of souls begins to increase, what assurance is there that we are not preparing a good meal for the devil? I am convinced that the safeguard lies in the cultivation of a certain attitude towards God, which in turn and by itself modifies one's attitude to oneself and to other people.

April 27, 1952 I question the implications of the idea that everything is material, because this suggests that there is no God, or at any rate implies that God is comparable or measurable against other and ordinary things. There is a fundamental fallacy in any system that does not place God at the central point.

April 28, 1952 It is interesting to me how attempts at new language seem to lead on the one hand to religious language and on the other to scientific, and beyond both perhaps there lies in the future a new language which will be a real compound of both.

May 4, 1952 Studying the physical and electromagnetic properties of light suggested the idea to me that light could be regarded as an instrument of divine intelligence, in the same way as a man's body of flesh and bones can be regarded as the instrument of human intelligence. If we try to imagine an intelligence attached to energy in the state of light, we find that such an intelligence would be omnipresent, everlasting, would contain within itself the possibility of transmutation into all kinds of more concrete forms, and so on. In other words it would answer to all the descriptions of divinity provided by different religions.

What we cannot analyse, of course, is the nature of an intelligence or being which could be manifested through light in this way. Intellectually and scientifically, as far as I can see, we can only study the instrument of divinity. To approach the being and intelligence of divinity, we probably have to go by another way.

Different lines of tradition and investigation put the emphasis in different places. There seems to be nothing wrong in this.

All different types of men have to be catered for, and the truth must appear in different forms and with different emphasis suitable to each.

As regards the ideas of spirit and matter, to me the idea of believing in one to the exclusion of the other would be the same as believing in the bottom of the ladder to the exclusion of the top. It is the whole ladder and the possibility of the ordered progress up this ladder of those who understand which interests me.

MAY 20, 1952 All work must bring us to the point where we really feel God as the centre of everything, everywhere and in ourselves. Then work becomes no longer effort but pure joy. At the same time, according to my own experience, it is most important not to insist on this, nor to talk much about it to anyone till the moment when he has to a certain extent realised it in himself. Otherwise it produces either a useless and dangerous resistance or a cheapening of the idea of God that can destroy both the feeling and its meaning. This realisation grows in silence.

OCTOBER 1954 I realised over many years that our work is not a substitute for religion. It is a key to religion, as it is a key to art, science and all other sides of human life. Only one must put this key in a lock and use it to open a door. Every man needs a religion, but our work enables him to find esoteric religion.

There are two great visions of truth. First of Hierarchy, of a ladder from rock to Christ up which we are all struggling, helped by those above, helping those below. Second, the vision of God, in Whom all live and move and have their being, Who embraces and penetrates all, Who is no nearer or farther in one place than in any other.

Our work tells us a great deal about the first vision, teaches us how to change our place upon that ladder. The second vision is much more mysterious, though true self-remembering shows us the way to it. Beyond a certain point, man must have both visions. The first is his day, the second his night. For the full realisation of these two visions, especially the second, we need religion. For since God is that which joins and embraces all men, they have to worship Him together.

By temperament, inclination, study, and by the country in which I have to work, I became a Roman Catholic. I had already anticipated this several years ago. It only needed the right moment and opportunity. For this time is a crossroads.

Other people, at the same crossroads, might join different religions, though it seems to me that Roman Catholicism has the greatest reserve of esoteric truth. In any case, whatever religion they chose, it would be the esoteric part which they joined. So there would be no contradiction between them. For the esoteric parts of all religions are connected, as our own tradition shows. The forms of religion are inside time—those living in time can choose what form they like. Beyond time, in the place from which our direction comes, there are no forms, there is only truth and understanding.

FEBRUARY 7, 1955 There is only one way to keep the system* pure—that is by becoming pure oneself. With that, it does not matter what words one uses, the system will be purely transmitted. Without that, one may remember every phrase by heart, and each will be corrupted.

To remember oneself, to become free from egoism, to be kind, to be understanding, to serve the Work and one's fellows, to remember oneself and find God—by what other means can one hope to keep the sytem pure?

The System is the key to every branch of human experience. Religion is the highest branch of human experience. If the system is used to unlock religion wonderful things can be found. Beyond the system is God. Religion is the study of being rejoined with God. But if the system is used to unlock religion, then it becomes a *conscious and understanding return to God.*

The system is a universal key. But a key lying on the table is nothing but a piece of metal of curious shape. Each person must find the door he wishes to open with it, then consciously take up the key and open that door. Otherwise better that he had never been shown the key.

What we call self is a phantom belonging to this time and this space. Beyond time light shines straight through it, showing that it has no real existence. Beyond time *we* have nothing to fear, *we* have nothing to worry about. We must strive to make connection with our spirit outside time*. Then its knowledge and certainty will enter this physical life within this passing time. Self-remembering makes this connection. In a moment of self-remembering, body, soul and spirit are all aligned. Understanding flows between them. This is why in a moment of self-remembering we have no sense of time, we have no fear, we have no doubt. Forget ourselves again and time, fear and doubt return. But in self-remembering they have no place. It is true freedom. By it we will come to spirit and to God.

FEBRUARY 23, 1955 Every living creature must alternately work and rest. If we find a new intensity of work, we must find a new intensity of rest, or we shall be burned out. On the esoteric way, the vision of the great ladder of ascent, up which we must all struggle, helped by those above, helping those below, represents the day's labour. If we really feel the tremendous tension which this involves, there is only one form of rest great enough to balance it. This is the vision of God everywhere, in everything, of ourselves and all others in God. This is the night's rest. And it is the only real rest.

FEBRUARY 25, 1955 As I see it, our tradition is not itself religion, any more than it is astronomy or art. It is the key to every branch of human experience, and especially to religion as the highest form of it. It is true that it has the quality of religion about it, because it is Truth. But at a certain point it seems that this is not enough. One needs a religion in the full sense of the word, and then one will use the tradition to open the esoteric side of that religion, leaving all the external contradictions on one side.

MARCH 12, 1955 Religion means the art of becoming consciously re-joined to God. But with the aid of the Work a man can go straight to the esoteric side of the religion he chooses. The religion he chooses is his own business, of course. I myself became a Catholic last year. I had been moving towards the Catholic Church ever since I went to France at the age of sixteen and made a bee-line for the cathedral in every city. But it is the esoteric side of Catholicism which interests me, and the esoteric sides of all religions are in harmony. There is no contradiction, for the Hierarchy* is one, and the esoteric sides of all religions were launched by it, as was the great experiment started through Ouspensky and Gurdjieff for our own time.

I belong to the Fourth Way*, and always will. It is a very special way, much more different from the other ways than most people realise. But it can enter everywhere, harmonise with the real side of everything. The creation of harmony is its task. I want to learn more, participate in harmony on a bigger and deeper scale.

MARCH 21, 1955 God is not the same as consciousness; God is not the same as the absolute. Because God is a sacred word which produces a sacred echo. Consciousness and absolute are not sacred words, and do not produce this vibration, which immediately connects us with the truth, and in the sense of which it is impossible to lie or fear.

The body is a very wonderful and beautiful instrument. But there is a key-phrase in *The Whirling Ecstasy** which we must never forget. It says simply: 'Leave thy body and come.' This is very important. It is very clear—everything is said there. It does not mean we have to forget our body. It won't prevent us from going to God. The body will take us to God or prevent us. It all depends on the use we make of it. We must make good use of it—but remember we have to leave it.

AUGUST 6, 1955 No one who has really begun to work on the Fourth Way* can leave it. They may stop on the way for a short or long time, but they can't leave it. Because it is the most complete truth. And our training in the Fourth Way enables us to go straight to the deepest side of religion.

The Fourth Way is the way of harmonising all sides of life, reconciling all truths. If it shows us how to bring conscious understanding to psychology, science, art and all the problems of practical and personal life, does it not show us how to come also to religion, which is the highest aspiration of the human mind?

We have so much to learn. And we have to learn everywhere and in every way. Yet at the same time, this is a purely individual question—different for everybody.

AUGUST 12, 1955 No one, either in or out of the Church, can persuade me that there is any contradiction between the guiding influence of the Catholic Church and of the Fourth Way. There is only one Inner Circle, only one Hierarchy; Christ is the head of it, and all revelations of truth come from it. It is only when those impulses are projected into this world that contradictions, conflicting dogma and persecution are created by men's misunderstandings. In their origin there is harmony and in so far as we can remake harmony between the manifestations here, we approach the source and receive help from it.

OCTOBER 3, 1955 The source of our inspiration is from a place where there are no religions, only truth. If we go 'through' a religion it is only so that we may appreciate that place more and rise more quickly towards it.

HIERARCHY*

JANUARY 15, 1948 Ordinary mind cannot comprehend a certain scale of truth. We are in the position of a man who says: 'How can I believe in the tails-side of a penny, if I already believe in the heads?'

Much knowledge was given by Mr Ouspensky about the different levels of men and divine man. But in order to understand this knowledge it is necessary for one's mind and one's whole being to change.

Evidently there is no possibility of regeneration without a teacher of supernormal level. That such teachers existed before Christ seems to be clear if one reads the Hindu Upanishads, the life of the Buddha, the Egyptian Book of the Dead, and some other writings that have come down to us. And yet it may be that Christ represented the highest level of teacher yet to come into the world, and thus brought new possibilities to mankind. How can we judge? All that we can say is that truth does not produce contradictions—only the deviousness of the human mind.

To struggle with these problems we need a great deal of knowledge—about the nature of the universe, and man's place and possibilities, and about the intermediaries between ordinary man and higher powers. Mr Ouspensky left us very much knowledge about these things.

NOVEMBER 3, 1949 Sometimes it seems that all our work is to create right connections, between us and the teachers, and between ourselves. If these connections are established on a certain basis, with understanding, and if negativeness and misunderstanding can be eliminated from them, then a kind of network is created which can be used by higher powers for the dissemination of their influence. Every misunderstanding and every criticism, both of teacher and of each other, creates a block, so to speak, preventing the passage of school influence further. If a misunderstanding occurs, it seems that great patience is necessary, to watch until the moment when understanding may be reopened, and at all costs to do nothing to deepen or fix a misunderstanding permanently.

Strange: did you ever think that fear makes time? More fear, more time, less fear, less time. No fear, no time.

April 7, 1950 The one really interesting fact, the one really interesting understanding, is of the actual existence of higher man and of miraculous possibilities. We need a lot of knowledge to get all that can be got from this understanding, and sometimes the understanding recedes behind the knowledge. But it is this understanding, this memory that is the beginning of everything.

July 20, 1950 Only one thing I cannot understand—'Now that we have no teacher . . .' If we ever had a teacher, we have one now. If we have not one now, did we ever have one? Real connection with higher man is not confined within time as we ordinarily count it, and to me the only use of all the mathematics and diagrams and quotations is to show just this. Surely it would have been rather funny if after the crucifixion the disciples had said, 'Well, now we have no teacher, what shall we do?'

September 23, 1950 It is my belief that Mr Ouspensky achieved a state in which he was not and is not confined to time as we are. Some of the implications of this I tried to develop in *Eternal Life*. Others will strike each individual person. But among others it must mean that such a man, directing from outside time, so to speak, can develop a plan of work involving people all over the world and covering scores or even hundreds of years. Everything that has happened since Ouspensky's death confirms my certainty that such a great plan is in fact being worked out. And that anyone who sincerely wishes has a place in it.

I always disliked and still do dislike the idea of 'communications'. For although such things are certainly possible from higher man they are inevitably understood wrongly, and immediately they are spoken about give rise to superstition in some and incredulity in others. And in due course the superstitious and the incredulous inevitably quarrel.

But I have to tell you a story. Not long after Ouspensky's death, I went into his bedroom and sat down there in a rather curious, superstitious mood. After a minute or two a voice in me—it could have been a memory of Ouspensky's voice—said with the chuckle which I also remember very well: 'You want a communication from the dead. Well, you won't get one!' All the same, I always listen carefully to such voices, for they nearly always have something interesting to say.

October 25, 1951 The universe is built on hierarchy. Who fights with hierarchy fights with God.

Group work is only possible if a smaller group within it takes more responsibility, works harder, demands more of themselves than the rest. This smaller group in turn is only possible if one or two take more responsibility still, push further towards the goal, press harder on the heels of their teacher and so lead the way.

November 17, 1951 Here suddenly come several letters saying that the idea of third force in self-remembering has come as a revelation. It seems to me that this is the key to what those who aspire to Christ or God are seeking. For true self-remembering is the consciousness of one's relation with another in the presence of a higher power. Our relation with each other stands in the presence of the Hierarchy, of which the head is Christ.

March 4, 1952 We have to find a 'para-psychology'. And I am sure that this can only come to us with help from higher levels, whether one takes this in an inner sense or as represented by higher man.

September 20, 1954 It is only recently that I have begun to realise the sublime importance of the relation of the Sun to the Fixed Stars. Evidently man's great hope and great salvation lie beyond the Sun. It is a wonderful vision.

AUGUST 14, 1955 It is clear as the sunshine that there is and always has been only one Inner Circle, one Hierarchy under Christ, which has brought man every good gift he has ever had. One feels the beings of that Hierarchy so near in every place that the sense of their absence becomes the only sadness.

AUGUST 16, 1955 I do not feel gloom in our situation—on the contrary, an immense and miraculous possibility, whose fulfilment depends upon our sensitiveness to the very special help which is now being made available to us from the hierarchy.

On the other hand, I see that Ouspensky had to go through utmost gloom in order to open a door through which new light should shine. I think not only individuals but also groups and whole esoteric experiments have to pass through the dark night of the soul, and the work of Ouspensky and Gurdjieff did so in those hard years before the war. Now it should be emerging into the light.

I also believe that Gurdjieff and Ouspensky were the two chosen agents of at least one stage of a new revelation. They were partners and complements, chosen because they represented and could transmit opposite aspects of the same truth. Two poles have to be separated for electric current to jump between them and make light. This was the reason for the separation of Gurdjieff and Ouspensky—it was by mutual agreement, to create a field of tension in which important preparations could be made.

SEPTEMBER 28, 1955 It is true that there is something behind our teaching; much more even than those who have studied for many years have guessed. There is the invisible influence of the Hierarchy.

OCTOBER 3, 1955 True humility is connected with giving up the luxury of worrying about ourselves. It makes no difference whether it is in the form of vanity about our achievements or doubts that we can do what is required of us. Both are preoccupation about ourselves, and pre-occupied with oneself one cannot see what is needed nor be open to receive the help which is pouring down upon us all the time, and which if we trust in it can enable us to do the impossible.

Love comes when we forget ourselves and feel other people, feel our Masters, feel God. Humility comes when we catch a glimpse of the great Work and great achievements, and see how infinitely small we are by comparison. It brings a great sense of freedom. Who does not feel humility when he is aware of his tiny body in relation to the mountain he is climbing, and who does not feel free and happy in that moment? Love and humility can't be invented and they can't be simulated.

OCTOBER 29, 1955 At first sight it seems a hard saying that none can progress alone but only in touch with School*. But when we begin to understand that the Inner Circle, the Hierarchy, is charged, under Christ, with the whole development of mankind, and that there is in fact only *one* Hierarchy and *one* Work, then the idea is not hard but tremendously satisfying. It means that if we also wish to enter the current of man's conscious development, we have to make contact somehow or other with those who are in charge of it. Whether this means physically, spiritually, or both physically and spiritually, is another question. But obviously it must be so.

I know that Ouspensky and Gurdjieff were and are members of that Inner Circle. I also know that if one's fate becomes attached to their fate, one shares their connection. But how can this be done? Chiefly by inner understanding and longing. At the same time if that understanding and longing is strong enough, one naturally wants to know and work with others going by the same path. Sooner or later one has to belong to a group, in order to widen one's understanding and speed up one's development. For whereas alone one can only acquire the understanding of one's own type and background, in a group—if it is a real and harmonious one—one can share in the understanding, experience and duty of many different types. Also, a sincere and unified group can attract help on quite a different scale from a lone individual. This is plain economics —and the celestial variety operates by similar laws to the human.

It means that one must become absorbed into a higher

organism, a greater magnetic field. A group should be that. But this does not mean that you have to see the other members of your group every day, or even live within a thousand miles of them. It means you must be innerly and organically connected with them and with the force which directs them. It is true that you may have for a while to work very intimately and physically with them, in order that this inner connection should grow strong. But when it is established, your duties may take you somewhere quite different without its being in any way weakened. For it is weakened only by doubt, denial, fear and vanity—never by physical or temporal conditions.

December 16, 1955 There is enciphered in *In Search of the Miraculous* almost everything one could wish to know about the work of the Inner Circle of Humanity and the conditions of our coming under their influence. But it is all in a kind of cipher, and when we come to experience these things, they will all have a strange and unexpected flavour. At the same time everything one can master from that book now will help one to orientate oneself more certainly later on. The influence of the Inner Circle is very real and immediate.

In this connection, the mi-fa interval* is of great interest. Because it is precisely at this interval that influence from a higher level can penetrate. In relation to our own lives such intervals are seen as crossroads, and what help reaches us at certain crossroads and how we react to it may affect our path very much in the future.

December 16, 1955 About abandoning the System. Even the greatest must go beyond themselves, as we all have to go beyond ourselves. They have to abandon the very forms they have created, in order to move up to new levels of freedom and understanding, just as we have to abandon the physical form which has served us so well in life, when we come to die. It doesn't mean that the System which Ouspensky developed won't serve others very well, but it does mean that those who are able must help release him by giving new life to what he left, rather than perpetuating it as a dogma.

In esoteric affairs, every understanding and reaction which

follows from higher influence, has its place and its use. Polarity and tension between different understandings there is and will be—that gives life and force, provided it does not become cruel and exclusive. We must keep our eyes and our hearts open, and try to see traces of the Great Plan everywhere, without judging too much.

I understand very well when people feel that their contact with the Work must have been for others and not for themselves. We all have that feeling when we glimpse its nobility and grandeur. At the same time that contact has been given us personally, and we must take the chance ourselves, for it was not for nothing that it came our way. We must understand that the awareness and influence of the Spiritual Hierarchy is not in some remote Shamballah, but penetrating our world and our life at every moment. At a certain degree of interest and longing one cannot help but attract their attention. Then it is very important to listen continually in one's conscience to what they have to suggest, and never again to lose that life-giving connection. We always have hope in Christ and His assistants, known and unknown.

MARCH 17, 1956 No one is alone—either in their troubles or in the help they receive. We need never be alone if we begin to understand what that means.

MARCH 19, 1956 It is possible to feel great harmony—the harmony projected from above within which all real work must take place. Without that feeling, we become lost in preoccupation with ourselves.

All inspiration and true teaching that ever came to man came from the same circle, the Hierarchy. If people understood that, there would be no more quarrels about different religions, philosophies or customs. Instead, they would begin to reflect the harmony which already exists *there*, where the Hierarchy works.

HARMONY

SEPTEMBER 7, 1955 I feel that 'harmony' is something which is actually being made possible for us now. A new secret, on a tremendous scale. The science and art of realising on earth what Christianity revealed in Heaven.

SEPTEMBER 24, 1953 I feel that we have very much to learn from the idea that a man, like a tree, can only grow upward as well as down—he is standing midway between. Down to reconciliation with the past, the instinctive, the underworld. It seems to me now that half the horrors of the last 2000 years arose from misunderstanding that man should climb kicking the ladder away behind him. That kicking away produced the Albigensian Crusade, the Inquisition, and God knows what other amputations, inner or outer. In the new beginning, this mistake must not enter. The answer lies in the law of harmony. Music shows how.

NOVEMBER 1, 1954 It is immensely important to create a wide understanding and harmony between many different kinds of people and many different lines. For the harmony which we achieve in ourselves, in our groups and between our groups, is the example of far greater harmony which has yet to be achieved. And this greater harmony in turn is the stage onto which a really great School demonstration will one day be launched.

It takes a long time to realise that our work is not a substitute for religion. Every man and woman needs a religion, to help him find direct connection with God. Outside time and space, all religions are one—one truth. But inside time and space, where we have to work, we must choose one, and find all truth there.

DECEMBER 2, 1954 The next thirty years are of crucial importance in the history of humanity and we need to co-ordinate evidence from all angles which will help us to understand what is at stake. An immense effort has to be made to achieve harmony between things which hitherto have been regarded as irreconcilable. Harmony—as a science and art, not as a sentiment—is the key task of our time. For only the achievement of real harmony will enable us to take the right turning at a big crossroads which lies ahead.

JANUARY 2, 1955 Everything is moving and growing so fast around us. Everything seems to be crying out, 'The new era is here—prepare for it, be ready, be ready!' I know that the key to the new era is 'harmony', and all that cannot be drawn into the harmony must be left behind. It is so clear that the tide is flowing towards us all who have been entrusted with some of the hope and certainty of Higher School. When people learn to forget themselves—how much there is for them to do! And what happiness in doing it!

MARCH 8, 1955 Everywhere people are expecting something new, feeling that something new is required of them. But they do not know what. The weaker ones drift into group imaginations that they will be carried by the tide to a new millennium. The stronger ones work on their own as best they can. And strangely enough it is especially those who immediately recognise Ouspensky's work for what it is, the true key to the new age. The others too like it when they hear, but then they try to approximate it with other cheaper things, and so lose their chance. In any case those who truly work for harmony immediately recognise each other. And it is upon their recognition that the great harmony grows.

SEPTEMBER 30, 1955 It has seemed to me that we must anticipate the time when there will again be a single science formed by the union of astrology and astronomy—that is, all the new knowledge of modern astronomy combined with the ancient understanding of celestial intelligence and celestial influence. It is one example of the great work of harmonising all the apparent contradictions of human experience and human knowledge, which is our task today. Very much may depend upon the degree in which man can imagine and project harmony in our particular age.

In ancient Egypt science, religion and craft formed one single body of knowledge—as it must do again eventually.

At the same time, it is clear that the Egyptian priests anticipated and prepared for the coming of Christ far in advance. Evidently at the incarnation, a break had to be made with the past, so that men should realise the magnitude of what had happened. For two thousand years there has been a kind of schism between the pre-Christian and the post-Christian world. As I say, I think it was necessary in order that men should realise that some quite *new* chance had come to the earth. But now I believe this division has to be healed. It has to be shown that all memorials of truth in all ages of the earth belong to the same plan, and come from the same source. It is the same work of harmony.

SEPTEMBER 30, 1955 I feel strongly that all those who are thinking in terms of the new harmony should know and recognise each other, at least by name and personally if possible. Their common recognition of each other and of a great plan far above them all makes a positive field of force in which many things are possible.

NOVEMBER 20, 1955 It is certainly a very interesting question about the higher meaning of 'democracy'. In relation to special work and special studies, it seems to me that the key of the new age is that knowledge, tasks and responsibilities are now given to groups rather than individuals. That was certainly what Gurdjieff and Ouspensky demonstrated, though they may not have said so explicitly. In fact it often seemed to me that all Gurdjieff's ideas about groups recorded in *In Search of the Miraculous* was not so much practical direction to his followers as the general blueprint for esoteric work in the age to come. It is very interesting in practice, because it means that among people related in this way, nobody can be allowed to get too far behind, nor can anyone get too remotely far ahead. They have to go forward together, as all parts of the body have to develop together, for real health and harmony.

In fact the key of such work in groups is precisely harmony. And this does seem to be the key-idea and the key-task of our age. It is not the period for those human meteors who soar off into the heavens, leaving everybody else behind. In this so-called 'democratic' age, I believe we do all sink or swim together, on many different scales. And it is only by finding the secret of harmony and equilibrium between all parts and influences, that we shall swim.

This indeed seems to be the great symbol which is to be realised on January 21 of next year [1956]. The extraordinary equilibrium of all the planets in this new cross—the Sun, Mercury and Venus in Aquarius over against Jupiter, Uranus and Pluto in Leo; Mars, Saturn and Neptune in Scorpio over against the moon in Taurus, this seems to be the arch-sign and promise of harmony for the age to come.

In fact, I believe that three dates taken together give us the clues we need about the transition to the new era. The last era was launched when the sun, representing Divinity, entered the Fish, and the earth, representing humanity, entered the Virgin; and it was confirmed when God, Whose symbol was the fish, and disciples fishermen, was born among men of a Virgin. In some way this new age must be inaugurated by Divinity assuming the new role of the Water-carrier, and humanity, this new role of the Lion. Surely the two dates—August 14, 1955, when the sun and six planets conjoin in Leo, and February 4, 1962, when the sun and six planets will conjoin in Aquarius, have something to do with fixing these new roles? And surely the reconciliation of the two is to be found precisely in the equilibrium of January 21, 1956? If all real things are created by triads of influences, then is it not possible that this triad of configurations is setting the mood of this world for a very long time to come?

It is interesting that the twenty-four cycles of Uranus and twelve cycles of Neptune take us back to the time of Christ. Will it not be this time as it was before, that the new influences must come to men simultaneously in two ways—mechanically and destructively on the one hand, and combined with divine intelligence and goodness on the other?

DECEMBER 27, 1955 It is extraordinary how the key-word of harmony occurs everywhere now, comes instinctively to everyone's lips when they wish to express what they hope for. But I feel that we have hardly yet begun to study its real meaning. Harmony is not an emotion, an effect. It is a whole elaborate science, which for some reason has only been fully developed in the realm of sound. Science, psychology and even religion are barely touching it as yet. Nor do I believe that there is any better understanding of it in the East than in the West. The passive abandonment to God may be still more familiar there, I do not know. But even that is only one chord in the harmony of all possible human attitudes and experiences, which must be created in our age.

I am not depressed about the West. There are traces of the new truth to be found everywhere—in books, in films, in speeches. The whole mood has changed incredibly in the last five or six years, as if in preparation for something. The East seems to me more disturbing because they have not yet found their way to *new* expression of the truth. What is best there is ancient and inert—I doubt if it can stand up to the tremendous strain of the changes which are working faster every day. Certainly the Sufi way seems more suitable for the West than the Far Eastern traditions. It was always more at home in the market place than in the ashram, and that is modern enough. How wonderful a new Mathnawi would be, written against the background of Western cities, with Western types and examples! On Jelaledin Rumi's tomb at Konya is a poem that goes something like this:

In a great invisible triumph,
In a tomb constructed of love,
Under a dome of living green,
Our lord sleeps in eternal wakefulness.

How well it would do for Ouspensky!

FEBRUARY 2, 1956 Music penetrates deep into people's being. Some of it comes from another world, trying to tell its hearers, and perhaps the composer himself, about things which cannot be told in words.

The conductor with his baton, the instrumentalists blowing and scraping, are inside time, moving along time. But obviously the great music exists even when no one is playing it.

So it must exist outside time. But what is music outside time? If we happen to catch that, is it not something which is not susceptible to improvement, something perfect and significant as it stands?

I have just been reading the Greek ideas about music. They are very interesting. Music for them was a way in which all parts of the organism could be united. It was supposed to contain three elements—*melos* or melody, developed in the throat; *rhythmos*, felt in the solar plexus; and *harmonia*, which was connected with the perception and the beating of the heart. These three elements, combining in the different ways, created the six or seven modes, which were an evocation of the six processes* we study. The chief instrument was the seven-stringed lyre, the centre string representing the sun, the three above the inner planets, and the three below the three outer ones.

Melos, rhythmos and harmonia, realised on these seven strings, made a true image of the interaction of the Law of Three and the Law of Seven*. This was and is the magic of music. Whether they understand it or not, musicians are imitating cosmic laws—and (with help) the strangest things may happen.

FEBRUARY 7, 1956 There is an enormous work to be done, giving the meaning back to all sides and studies of modern life, which have completely lost their relation to the whole. If we have been given this very special key, it is so that we may really begin to create harmony, physical, emotional and intellectual, in new fields.

MARCH 1, 1956 I always like to imagine the total effect of the work of Gurdjieff and Ouspensky in the present world, influencing every country and aspect of modern life through a dozen groups and thousands of individuals. I think it is much more powerful than we imagine, and that its work is to give an example of harmony. In that case, every encounter becomes important as a proof of the success or failure of that example.

THE WORK

MARCH 14, 1947 Reading a story by Stephen Vincent Benet about a primitive priest in the far distant future rediscovering the ruins of New York, then a review of Toynbee's enormous history of the world with its rise and fall of twenty-six civilisations, and then just opening the newspaper to the current news—for a while I had such a vivid sense of our time, the whole structure of our civilisation swaying more and more wildly, everything crumbling and tottering, and yet even as it crumbles a few men perched on its highest point suddenly seeing staggering views on a scale that has never been possible before—far back into the earth's history, far across the starry nebulae, far into the minutest structure of matter, atoms and molecules. It is not them—it is just because the whole world stands on the edge of a precipice that these secrets are revealed to them; just as in the war when the house next door to you was bombed out of existence, instead of a dirty wall six feet from your bedroom window, you might suddenly wake up to a clear view of St. Paul's, miles away in the distance.

What then, in the middle of all this, is the Work, the system*? Which is the same at the beginning of an age, or the climax of it, or the end. Which at bottom has nothing to do with such a cycle at all, but shows a way out of it—at right angles, so to speak, the only possible way out of the wreck.

JUNE 30, 1948 A weakness also implies a corresponding capacity, and at a certain point individuals are required to transmute their weakness into a talent. Since they have nothing else, it is their only chance of becoming useful. So somehow people must learn to rise above their ordinary doubts about themselves. Preoccupation with one's weakness is the last form taken by self-importance. It sounds beautiful, but it is precisely this which prevents people from seeing the larger issues, after they may have successfully struggled with more obvious obstacles.

No one is prepared; no one ever is. Work is work, and from

a larger point of view it is merely a question of who will try to do what is required. The delicacy of the excuse is not taken into account, if we are to believe the parable of the wedding guest.

AUGUST 1948 I am sure that more is now possible than ever before—both for Mr Ouspensky's work as a whole, for small groups, and for individual people who remember him, and experiment as best they can. *Provided* also they realise that the plan of a great work has already been created, and our task is not to invent work but to strive to understand and manifest his. Yet to do this we have to remember everything—him, his work, ourselves, and the connection between them.

JANUARY 14, 1949 One has to wait without impatience for what should come, and yet at the same time do everything within one's power as though one were impatient and as though one were solely responsible. I believe that a great plan was conceived, and awaits realisation, so to speak. But I also believe that its fulfilment must be *through* relatively ordinary people like ourselves becoming sensitive enough to respond to hints and demands which are too subtle to be ordinarily noticed, and making ourselves carry out whatever is innerly perceived. If many people begin to do this, I believe they can between them be instrumental in the working out of a plan far greater than any single person can conceive.

I do not believe any higher plan will or ever can fulfil itself by a kind of violation of cosmic laws, without the understanding and intense co-operation of those who are in a position to help. In some way difficult to define a kind of active anticipation is necessary—seeing what atmosphere would be necessary for higher intervention and scrupulously doing everything which will help to create it.

This in turn seems to be something to do with a different perception of time, which exists somewhere in us. I believe that somewhere within us, we have been given to know or guess very much of the future of our work—but our ordinary mind can't quite catch it, except in a very special state. So that we are left only with the vague sense that something unusual *should* happen. Yet I think this same sense can tell us very well what is favourable to this unknown 'future'—what actions and connections, what payment of debts, what common understanding and positive attitude, what desire to master all sides of life, are needed.

Something seems to work in such a great impersonal way, both on an immensely noble scale and on a daily trivial one, with such magnificent alternation of passive and active aspects—that somehow I cannot bring myself to take very seriously all the personal individual heartsearchings and fears and hopes that we have been accustomed to associate with the Work.

Certainly they too must have their place. Yet receiving many letters one begins to recognise what we have come to call the 'humility clause'—when having understood and expressed something rightly, people hurry to disclaim any responsibility for it by dragging in all kinds of qualifications about imagination, not being able to judge, not being able to do, things being beyond their understanding, and all the rest of it. With some people all the strength of what they have understood seems to be neutralised by such qualifications, which pass for humility, but to me look more like a desire not to be held responsible for what they know. I firmly believe that the only way to get beyond a certain point is to accept responsibility up to the hilt for what, in fact, one knows very well indeed. The whole of Ouspensky's life, from the days of *Tertium* and earlier, seems to have been based on taking almost outrageous responsibility for things he knew, but which a more timid man would argue himself out of.

FEBRUARY 10, 1949 When a man breaks a new way into higher worlds* (and I believe that Ouspensky's achievement was the opening of a new way that did not exist before, or at least the redeeming of an old way) he seems to do so partly on the momentum of those who follow him. If he has taught well, the emotions he has aroused help to lift him, so to speak. They give him flight. Those who believe in him become part of his work, and he in turn becomes responsible for them.

All this used to be put very simply in the explanation about the staircase, where no step can remain empty, but all must move up together. It is a great whole which must move, and the whole forms the work of the man who leads, and who has already broken through. Ouspensky moved up. Now all connected with him must also move, the whole must move.

Evidently this whole, this work, must exist outside time*. And it is clear that once one becomes seriously part of such a work, it is for all time and all eternity; all one's possibilities and responsibilities lie within that work; and even if one remains alone, seeing no one, still one is indissolubly joined to everyone else who is part of that work, and one shares in the greater fate.

All his life Ouspensky created right causes, which went echoing all over the world, touching many and most unlikely people on the way. He could not while alive reap all the effects of these causes, but it may happen that in some cases we can. And all this seems to be our real work, developing the ideas he left in outline, the plans he only suggested, the lines of work he hinted, the contacts he established, but could not complete. Perhaps our best way of preparing for next time is by accepting such unfinished business as our own. Of course fates and capacities are different, but if he remains alive to possibilities, I think each person must come across such loose ends which his conscience tells him are his business. This is what I mean by the sense of Ouspensky's work as a whole.

April 3, 1949 As soon as one begins to feel that Ouspensky's work and achievement were not in our time, which seems to pass, but in a different dimension of time altogether, it becomes clear that all those who were once really connected with Ouspensky always will be connected with him—and with each other.

There are many strange analogies in music with such work existing outside time. A man writes a symphony. A conductor collects an orchestra of many instruments and gives a performance. The music is actualised in one place at one particular day and hour. The manuscript may then lie lost in a drawer for years, even centuries. One day it is found. Another conductor collects another orchestra. The music is again actualised, in another place and at another moment in time, which bear no relation to the first at all—and yet if it is the same music, it produces the same emotions in players and audience. And the number of times and places in which it may be played is infinite, but the result is always the same or similar. The symphony itself somehow exists outside time and place, but it can be evoked again whenever the right players with the right conductor get hold of a copy of the score.

In some way, I feel that the 'score' of our work exists somewhere outside time. Ouspensky got hold of this score, and without many people realising what was happening he got his players together and after coaching them for a long time in the theory of music, he actually put on a performance. That performance can be placed and dated in our time. But because it is an actualisation of the symphony itself, it also exists outside our time, and can always be reproduced in greater or lesser part by those who have the skill, knowledge and particularly *memory* of the last performance. Even individual players may whistle some of the tunes; what I mean is that all that is miraculous in our work—and that is all that matters—exists outside time.

MAY 31, 1949 Sometimes I feel that all our work is to make connections. If we can make and strengthen our inner connection with Ouspensky's people all over the world, and swallow the misunderstandings that prevent inner connection, and if this network of connections is in turn connected with Ouspensky, then an immense force can flow through the whole and express itself equally in any part and any place.

NOVEMBER 1, 1949 All this that one was shown seemed to be quite incommensurable with oneself, one's own efforts, hopes and so on—only immense, incalculable good fortune. And I understand now why Mr Ouspensky used to speak about 'luck'—that 'luck' cannot be left out. For what we were given was quite incommensurable with all that we ourselves were, or even could be, capable of. Strangely, this understanding that one can never deserve what one is aiming for, makes things very close and attainable, which before seemed impossibly far off. It changes one's whole point of view about everything.

As to the present, and the future, the same time showed that a great plan develops, hidden behind all that we see, and that all of us, by our merely having come under a certain influence, have a relation to this plan. So that perhaps all we have to do is simply not to hinder the working out of this plan, not to set up causes which go against it, and to neutralise the wrong causes that hinder us now. It seems sometimes that all we have to do is first to swallow our own negativeness, and then to swallow other people's. How much poison can one swallow? Perhaps that's all there is to it.

FEBRUARY 22, 1950 More and more it seems to me that a tremendous effort is being made by some force behind the scenes to unite in understanding—(not externally)—all people everywhere who have reached a certain level, and who can take part—(even without knowing it)—in the unfolding of some new possibilities on a very large scale indeed. Perhaps this tremendous effort of growth is exactly proportionate to the equally tremendous dangers that face mankind. But I feel it more and more, because so many interesting things happen, so many connections are made, and so many possibilities open up, that not only are far beyond anything we could calculate or hope for, but also in some way beyond the circle of influence that one would expect of any single teacher, however great. As though there were some deep inner co-operation on a very high level between what for centuries have been separate lines of growth.

MARCH 27, 1950 In the light of a certain big achievement, big plan, one has to disappear. One's personal self, with which one lives nearly the whole time, is too small to have any relation to that. So it has to disappear, if one is to understand. The more it disappears, the more can be understood.

This may be very painful—for a time. Later, it is quite the reverse; and it is the return, the interference of the personal self which becomes painful, and its absence happiness.

There are two sides of our work and they must go together. The first is the gradual weakening and the end destruction of this false side, this personal self, which at present arranges our lives. The other is the gradual acquirement of something new, a new permanent guiding principle of consciousness, which we have not got at present. We have to lose something we have, and create something we have not. Giving up self-will shows the way towards the first, self-remembering the way towards the second.

JULY 9, 1950 I think the sense of the complete unimportance of all one's personal life and personal psychology is the key to entry into relation with some invisible esoteric stream. To me this has no taste of humility or self-abasement; it is simply that one's life as an 'independent' person ceases to have any meaning, and therefore there is no more point in being humble about it than proud of it. Pride and humility seem two sides of the same state—of taking oneself as an individual seriously.

DECEMBER 27, 1950 For me more and more becomes clear by striving to see our whole work in all parts of the world and in all its duration of time, as one thing. Unity and pattern in fact exist. 'We are members of one body, members one of another', as the first Christians said. If we say 'functions' instead of members it accords better with our language—and functions are very different, and must become *more* distinct, even while better serving and understanding the whole.

APRIL 20, 1951 To me it is the sense of a great plan that reconciles the 'vision' of all and the 'vision' of contradictions. For the all—indeed the work of higher school*—contains a great plan. Seen as a whole this plan is unity; seen in its details, some contrasting with others, it looks like contradiction. It is only a different focus, as when you look through a window and focus on the whole vast view beyond; or focus on the window-pane and see individual rain-drops and specks of dust.

To me, more and more, the apparent contradictions, apparent struggle—if one simply swallows them—seem each to be symbolic of a different part of the plan, which may be too vast to be grasped whole, and only visible in these paradoxical parts.

And attention is the only practical way to reconcile the two views, bring them together.

NOVEMBER 14, 1951 In this work it is right that all points of view should be considered; that right traces be left, that all be decent and in good taste, and that an atmosphere of love and friendliness be created. But behind all that is a force a thousand times more powerful, which when released can tear mountains apart, transform crucifixions, and split our everyday world from top to bottom. And in the light of this, the first will disappear like a candle in the sun.

NOVEMBER 15, 1951 My aim is to live permanently in this miraculous atmosphere, or at least permanently in the knowledge and memory of it.

At such times it is less and less the need of *personal work* I feel, and more and more the urgency of acting as a pure and understanding instrument in the realisation of a great plan. To me this means scrupulously right action in relation to every individual and every situation concerned, firmness when firmness is required, gentleness when gentleness, and so on. It means right action in relation to individuals, to groups, to whole lines of work. Collin-Smith simply does not enter into it. He is not of sufficient interest. But if what is then understood as necessary to the plan is scrupulously carried out, that provides all the work Collin-Smith needs or requires. This is what I mean by less and less importance attached to personal work. The focus has to shift elsewhere, and the rest will take care of itself.

I believe it a kind of blasphemy, when great things are being revealed or required, to say: 'Please pay attention to *me*, Collin-Smith', and I think that attitude is left over from the great illusion of I. If that illusion dies, then personal work goes up in smoke. There is no such thing.

This feeling colours very much my idea of physical demands. Certainly physical demands will include such things as fasting, holding out arms, getting up in the night to do some exercise, and so on, to keep oneself sensitive and in training, so to speak. It also includes, I believe, such tasks as keeping oneself quite motionless for a definite time or continuously moving for a definite time. In fact, *any* action of the body carried far beyond its normal duration becomes a physical demand. But beyond all that, physical demand means to me that one should demand of one's physical body that it become a pure instrument of the compassion of school. That demands should be made upon it to soothe, heal, stimulate, shock or fortify others, as the Work demands. This means that the old shrinking from contact or longing for comfort of the old body of Collin-Smith must be transcended, and that it be demanded that it does whatever is required, fully and freely. For in relation to physical demands, as to all else, I hear Ouspensky's voice saying: 'But why? That is the question.'

I believe much could be done from the point of view of making the body a pure instrument for all manifestations that are required of it—how to be a pure warrior, a pure craftsman, a pure lover of God, and corresponding roles for women's bodies too. We do not yet know how to require of our bodies at will to be fierce, devout, compassionate, meticulous or tender. But this is what we have to learn, before we can serve school fully and impersonally.

NOVEMBER 22, 1951 I feel very deeply that Ouspensky's work as a whole is nearing new realisations, nearing a more direct awareness of influence from higher powers. And I feel that very much of the work of the last three years has been gradually to melt away old obstacles and resistances to the entrance of the miraculous.

Ouspensky's work must be nourished by divinity, by the influence of great school, the influence of the inner circle of humanity, and by him personally as representative to us of all these things. But how can we receive this nourishment?

About two years ago I began to realise very strongly that self-remembering*—which was always put as the very key of our way—must like every other phenomenon be the product of three forces. The old double-headed arrow showed us how divided attention gives awareness of two of these three forces simultaneously—myself and the world around me. But what is the third without which the true state of self-remembering cannot manifest? It seemed to me that it was the remembrance of myself and that other simultaneously existing in the presence of some higher power, simultaneously bathed in some higher influence, simultaneously bathed in the light of the sun, if you like.

It became clear that it was difficult to speak about this third force, for to each person it will appear in different guise—the teacher, the teaching, an ideal, the sun, God. But in any case, it will be a force from a higher level which equally embraces both of the other factors.

Earlier this year the phrase from St. John's Gospel made a very strong impression on me: 'Whatsoever ye shall ask the Father in my name, he will give it you.'

Among the many extraordinary impressions at the time of Ouspensky's death there was—particularly at one period—the immensely strong feeling of some great power or being, some Christ-like being, as far above Ouspensky as Ouspensky was above us, presiding over all that was being done. The whole chain of ascent which was written about in the last chapter of *Eternal Life* was not an idea only, but something which could then be sensed in fact. I think it is this which can nourish us. And I believe the first step to such new nourishment is the realisation of Ouspensky as a living force, the permanent intermediary between ourselves and the highest powers, through whom all things can be asked.

It interests me very much that new people begin to speak and ask more and more in religious language, and less and less in psychological. At the same time I see that scientific knowledge is the special capacity of our age. But it seems to me that scientific knowledge and religious understanding are on the point of meeting, the two languages are just about to fuse. And that when they do, the true form of the new age will begin to develop.

The fanatic is one who already has certainty, but incomplete understanding. He has seen the goal, but not all the landscape between. As he sees wider he will lose his fanaticism.

JANUARY 7, 1952 It is a law that if the teacher rises, the pupils can rise also. By the special relation of teacher to pupil in school, they can share his achievement. We do not yet guess to what level Ouspensky has risen; so I think we have hardly begun to sense what opportunities and possibilities that rise implies for us. It means we have to expect more, ask more. For probably what we ask is now available.

MARCH 6, 1952 In life one can say anything but in Work one cannot speak if one has not made at least some effort in relation to what one speaks about. Only when one knows this, life becomes Work, and so after all there is no difference.

MARCH 13, 1952 The enneagram* is a pattern, the model of a cosmos. Every cosmos contains all possibilities, including that of regeneration. And individual man is a cosmos, but lacks the knowledge and strength to realise this regeneration in himself. The earth also is a cosmos, but any process of regeneration which develops in relation to the earth, being on a geological time scale, is much too slow to be able to benefit a man with a lifetime of only eighty years.

For this reason the work of Great School is to create an *artificial* cosmos, halfway between the scale of man and that of the earth, and within which each participant can share in this regeneration on a new scale. The creation of such a cosmos is a task almost inconceivable to us. But we know for certain that it is according to the model of the enneagram. Understanding the enneagram, even in an elementary form, one begins to understand the form of the Christian drama.

MAY 20, 1952 At a certain moment one inevitably reaches the conclusion that this Work is the only one that is worth doing. Then everything else becomes important only in proportion to the extent to which it prepares for or helps or supports this Work. Later still one realises that nearly everything—in any case, everything *normal* can become affiliated with, and related to the main work. In the fourth way*, the more inner work is deepened the wider external work should become, and the more external work widens, the deeper internal work should become.

It is a principle that harmonised development means equal development in all dimensions. But this is a long-time principle and every stage has its given time and every moment its own lesson and special opportunity.

This is connected with the law of octaves*. These octaves sound through our lives and our association with the Work. And what is important is to make ourselves sensitive to the note which is sounding at the moment and respond to it. Much suffering in human life results from a fruitless attempt to retain a note that has already ceased to sound, or to anticipate a note that has not yet sounded.

June 16, 1952 I don't think a person need worry about having no apparent leader. If one has become really connected with such a leader, one is always so connected. As for the rest, someone said to Ouspensky in 1947: 'I know I am a machine and that I cannot work by myself.' He answered: 'Who told you that? Do not believe anyone who tells you that.' Someone else asked: 'Can one then learn in one's own case?' He said: 'Yes, certainly. *Only* in your own case. You can learn only for yourself.'

June 16, 1952 The phrase from *In Search of the Miraculous* about a man becoming free from the law of accident when he meets a representative of school, is a very strange one. Evidently it has many meanings, but one of them must be that schools are under different laws from ordinary life, and that a man who comes in touch with them is immediately affected by these new laws. Whether to his advantage or disadvantage will depend on his own being. In any case a testing process which in the accidental conditions of life could go on for scores of years is suddenly speeded up and becomes intentional and inescapable.

July 16, 1952 I sometimes see the whole series of books which have come out of the Ouspensky-Gurdjieff influence—from *Tertium Organum* on—as a single chain, which only in its totality contains the explanation of that influence.

DECEMBER 16, 1952 It is a sin to reveal miracles that happened to and through one in connection with one's own name and personality; it is equal or greater sin to fail to proclaim the glad tidings and to proclaim them in the only way possible—on the basis of one's own experience. What is the way out? Only, I believe, to put oneself completely in the hands of higher power—to be happy to be silent, to be happy to testify, to be happy that others are helped by one's testimony, to be equally happy that it be destroyed, misunderstood or turned against one. What does it all matter, provided that the great plan can work itself out freely through us?

JANUARY 2, 1953 Sometimes I feel that we are all being hurried along by some higher power as fast as we can manage, and that many of the things which look to us difficult are more like a sharp kick in the rear administered to those who want to hang behind. Something seems to be saying: 'Hurry, hurry!' 'Very difficult times,' we say. If we saw a little more, we would probably thank Heaven.

I see one thing interesting in connection with this hurrying on. The new lessons and moves are not difficult. What does make difficulty are the lessons we were supposed to learn way back, and failed to do so. They come back at us each round with renewed kick, until they are understood.

JANUARY 19, 1953 When a person reaches the point where he makes an interior decision to study seriously and with continuity, the possibility of turning back disappears. At the same time we find ourselves still surrounded by the circumstances and limitations of our past life. Everyone finds himself in this situation on entering this way. It has to be so for everyone who undertakes these studies, although the accumulated difficulties are very different for each person.

JANUARY 19, 1953 On this road one always feels that one has scarcely reached the point where one finds oneself. All the same, this 'scarcely' is not pessimistic. One can admit with real happiness that one has 'scarcely' reached something compared with the ever more immense horizons that open before one. In fact, this feeling of 'scarcely' is like a guarantee of safety at each step of the way. Personally I hope never to lose it.

JUNE 6, 1953 I am sure that the possibility of big change depends on one's nearness to Big School. It is like a great whirlpool with what Ouspensky was and is and what stands behind him at the centre. Beyond this vortex of esoteric energy the water is still. On its edge the water begins to swirl, slowly here and there changes are possible. The nearer the centre the faster the torrent, the quicker and more complete the transformation of an individual life. Nearer the middle, it seems to me, everything is in flux, anything is possible.

But to approach the vortex means to be drawn into the pattern of a great esoteric work. And the transformation of one's life which may follow will be only to enable one to play one's part more purely and rightly as that work needs.

JUNE 25, 1953 If we really understood what the word 'service' implies, many things would already be very different for us. All the work of the Inner Circle of Humanity is contained in it.

JULY 8, 1953 There comes a moment in which one becomes mortally tired of the idea of working on oneself, to free oneself personally from oneself. One feels a great longing for the great work of school, the enormous effort that the Inner Circle sends out for the real good of humanity. Ouspensky was a man who at the end faced the tremendous task without illusions.

JULY 9, 1953 Things are moving faster and faster, as it would seem to specks of dust caught on the surface of a whirlpool and being drawn ever more quickly towards the centre. Everybody has to forget habit. It is as though the chains of what people were and expected themselves and others to be, were being struck off, and a voice saying: 'Be free. Why not?' Only the freedom is not for their own amusement, but so that they may serve the great Work with all heart and soul and skill untrammelled.

JULY 14, 1953 Evidently there is a great new vision which *must* get itself expressed in the world at this time, through as many channels and in as many ways as possible.

JULY 24, 1953 I believe that our doubts and cares and clever carefulness are the one factor which prevents an inconceivably miraculous flowering of Ouspensky's work. I say this, because I can no longer shut my eyes to the fact that with every reservation that falls away, new and disproportionately wonderful things come about.

It was put into our hands to be the agents of miracles. And we tell people to control the expression of their negative emotions, not to push, and to form an orderly queue for an unknown bus, which may one day take them a twopenny stage nearer heaven! I wonder that a great voice doesn't come out of heaven thundering: 'O ye of little faith!'

When will people understand that a new age has really dawned? When will they stop sealing up the terrible crack into heaven which Ouspensky has made, with precautions and good behaviour? We must allow divine madness to take possession of us now, before hell freezes!

SEPTEMBER 7, 1953 In each age a great esoteric plan is set for the whole of humanity and in any given period stands at a certain phase of realisation. At the present moment we find ourselves between the conception and birth of a new plan. A real artist is one whose work has begun to reflect or harmonise with some aspect of the plan. This may happen unconsciously by sheer whole-hearted devotion to one's line. Or it may happen consciously, when a person begins to understand the nature of the plan, and the conditions of men's participation in it.

The more a person comes to understand the meaning of what is being attempted, the more his work will be filled with the meaning. If and when this happens, his work becomes incommensurable with any 'art' which he or anyone else can subjectively invent.

SEPTEMBER 7, 1953 Perhaps it is only when one's teacher

passes into the higher world, that he is able to transmit to us the 'grace' which makes actually possible for us what previously was only an aspiration. To be drawn fully into the Great Plan, we have to have a confederate and director in that world.

SEPTEMBER 24, 1953 All work for the creation of groups on earth is concerned with the building of arks to be navigated from a higher level. But my experience is that navigation may be far more exact and meaningful after the Teacher achieves and dies. For then he sees farther and wider; yet his work must still be with the ark he made. For that is both his karma and his means of expression. The difference is like navigating with a great captain, and then navigating under the first mate with radio.

OCTOBER 3, 1953 Love comes when we forget ourselves and feel other people, feel our Masters, feel God. Humility comes when we catch a glimpse of the great Work and great achievements, and see how infinitely small we are by comparison. It brings a great sense of freedom. Who does not feel humility when he is aware of his tiny body in relation to the mountain he is climbing, and who doesn't feel free and happy in that moment? Love and humility can't be invented and they can't be simulated. They are just the result of feeling more and seeing more.

MAY 24, 1954 It now seems to me that all those twenty years of spiritual austerity and slow grinding psychological work between the wars had one purpose. It was to generate the power and one-pointedness necessary so that at a certain point a tremendous break-through should be possible, to make a connection with higher worlds and Higher School. That point was Ouspensky's death. In fact, what had been planned was achieved. He did break through, restored the highest connection.

But this means that his own break-through leaves a crack through which his people can follow, if they understand and can become free from doubt and fear. At one of his last meetings in London in the spring of 1947, someone said despondently: 'I know that I am a machine and can do nothing by myself . . .' He shouted: 'Who told you that? Don't believe anyone who tells you that!' It means that we must believe in the possibility of work everywhere in all circumstances, in groups or alone, on one line or another line. *Because higher help is now available which was not available before.* And this in turn because he reached a new level, with quite different powers and quite different relations to time and space.

I think we have to go back to all the old material—*In Search of the Miraculous*, Dr Nicoll's *Commentaries* and so on—from quite a new point of view, with the conviction that all this *is actually realisable now*. Gradually it is absorbed into one, and oneself absorbed into it, the ideas become part of oneself. We must become more sensitive to new understandings, and carry the living memory of them through into ordinary life.

This means that one will see oneself more and more objectively, as we sometimes see a stranger on the street and suddenly know exactly what he is like and why. But without any blame or judgement, without self-pity or self-praise. Gradually comes the possibility of swallowing oneself—just as one is. Then one is ready for the big work.

May 30, 1954 When one takes one big new intentional step in life, many other things which seemed difficult and ominous before, begin to smooth themselves out. The main step may be very difficult, but this in itself may make secondary things easier.

August 11, 1954 I know that there is a Conscious Direction, both for all aspects of our special work, and also touching people and activities in a far wider field than we ever dreamed. To me, this Conscious Direction comes from Higher School, of which Gurdjieff and Ouspensky were and are agents—the two poles, perhaps, of a new world.

I feel that groups are like different functions of this new creation. Some functions may be more developed and others less; some are more sure of their own line, others still groping for it. But all are surely organic parts of a whole, which is using their special characteristics and understandings for its own ends. And only in relation to the whole can individual groups be seen in their right place and proportions.

AUGUST 14, 1954 Why do people spend so much time and energy trying to find a catch in things? Perhaps there is no catch. The Work goes on, great things are being created, with us and in spite of us. A cathedral is being builded. Which is more important—the Architect's plan or the fact that a certain foreman was too lazy or too harsh, or came to work drunk on Monday morning? Which of us in this Work can afford to be offended?

DECEMBER 28, 1954 We have such help to become free to serve the Great Work if we are prepared to forget ourselves and give everything we are and have to serving—to serving others, to serving Ouspensky and his friends, to serving God. When we really give ourselves to that, we see that our faults and failings are so small, so unimportant, almost as unimportant as our virtues! To give, to serve, to be kind, to love men, our teachers, the angels, and God. What more do we want? What more do we expect? What less dare we demand?

We must get over our doubts and fears and difficulties, our self-importance. All this has to go, and it will be taken from us if we sincerely wish, and if we do not cling to it—cling to our little selves. We have to become free as Ouspensky to go up, up, and up. Geoff* did that. He asked nothing for himself, he gave away everything he had, and then spent himself making things to give away also. When he died one could feel his spirit shooting upwards like a rocket—because there was nothing to hold him to this earth except his love to help his friends here —and the higher he goes the better he can do that.

DECEMBER 28, 1954 What for me emerges ever more clearly is our main line of development forward into the future and upward out of time. I feel that those of us who have been entrusted with so much by Ouspensky and Gurdjieff and Nicoll have to progress in these two dimensions simultaneously. We have to go forward into the future, knitting up knowledge and understanding on a wider and wider basis, projecting confidence and harmony around us on all scales, preparing for a great opportunity which is to come. At the same time we have to move upwards to greater and greater freedom and closer and closer connection with those who have prepared us in the past and are still leading us from outside time. We have to strengthen the link between the invisible Inner Circle of humanity and this physical life in which we individually have our sphere. There is so much to do. So much which is being given as celestial influence and has to be carried by us into human manifestation.

All types and qualities are needed in this performance, both in groups and those scattered on their own about the world. By finding *himself*, his own possibilities, each person finds his role in the Great Work. It is all connected with achieving food for the sun* and liberation for man. Connections beyond the sun too.

FEBRUARY 7, 1955 All over the world, people feel themselves on the brink of a new age, with new possibilities, and with the hope of a new kind of help from the Inner Circle of humanity, at the moment when men's unaided efforts so obviously can do nothing.

FEBRUARY 7, 1955 The book is called *The Theory of Celestial Influence* because what is written *is* only the theory of our possible transformation, our dying to an illusion and our passing under great and high powers which need us as understanding and selfless agents of their plan. The book is theory. We have to accomplish this transformation in ourselves—with help. But to anyone who really wishes it in their heart, this help is available no matter where they may be and what their circumstances.

It is very wonderful to see the seeds of a new future being sown. But the new era is not only for one continent. It is for the whole earth.

Nobody will be carried into the new era by the tide. It has to be struggled for, prepared for everywhere. The preparation is the creation of conscious harmony—first in oneself, and then projected into one's surroundings. The rest is not in our hands.

FEBRUARY 11, 1955 The *whole* Work is really a cosmos*—everything in it depends on and explains everything else. It is only when one catches a glimpse of the whole that one feels an enormous wonder at a great purpose.

MARCH 7, 1955 Some enormous plan is unfolding around and through us. A very great plan indeed, connected with preparation for a new era, on the eve of which we now find ourselves. Mr Ouspensky took responsibility for a very important part of this plan. The help is needed of all his friends in it, as much as they are able to make themselves sensitive to his influence and to their own fate and conscience. Each person has to find himself, be sincere, honest and truthful through self-remembering. Then he will gradually find his place in this plan, and all the help he can receive.

MARCH 21, 1955 If we really understood about different levels*, the whole idea of the Great Work would be clear to us. The ladder of ascent is like a rising octave. Any note upon it must sound with a note above and a note below to make a chord. But there are many different chords which go to make the great music. And in each chord we have a different relationship both with those above us and those below.

I myself have always felt a strong need to make our work connect right through to the simplest kind of people. We are trying to make a lightning conductor to attract celestial lightning. Every lightning conductor must be earthed—otherwise a strike will burn it out. The earthing of our work is by carrying it down to simple people in a form sincere enough and real enough to cater to their needs.

MARCH 23, 1955 It is difficult to write more about what is before us. It seems most true when one writes poetically, and that I tried to do in *The Herald of Harmony*. If one tries to make one's understanding factual, it escapes. I only know that we are preparing for a great demonstration from Higher School, the greatest since the time of Christ, that Mr Ouspensky and his companions have great responsibility for these preparations, and that for us individually, it means we must become completely free to serve, in body, soul and spirit . . . free of all fears, free of all longings, free of all regrets, free of everything that binds us to the earth, except what love of the Work and love of God gives us to do here.

July 20, 1955 The aim of the Work is to become free, and to help others to become free—free to serve a higher purpose.

What makes for freedom? Faith, kindness, courage, knowledge, selflessness, and understanding. This is the work of Schools. And the devil's work is to undermine it. He's very ingenious. The other day someone said to me: 'Isn't there danger of the system being corrupted by the virus of good works?' Who invented that charming phrase, if not the devil? Ouspensky's short story 'The Well-Meaning Devil' is very interesting.

October 3, 1955 True humility is connected with giving up the luxury of worrying about ourselves—it makes no difference whether it is in the form of vanity about our achievements or doubts that we can do what is required of us. Both are preoccupation about ourselves, and preoccupied with oneself one cannot see what is needed nor be open to receive the help which is pouring down upon us all the time, and which if we trust in it can enable us to do the impossible.

October 3, 1955 People must not worry that they seemed to have missed Ouspensky when he was alive. This influence is certainly as near us now as it ever was then, and I am constantly struck by the fact that many individuals who write to me often seem to have contacted the true Ouspensky more than others who spent twenty years of physical life with him.

October 24, 1955 All true messages are the same, come from the same place. What is being transmitted is very great, but we catch only one interpretation of it and think that is the whole. Yet we have to do that too, and no doubt will be shocked and pummelled until our vision reaches the scale that is needed.

If we have heard the authentic voice of higher help speaking through another person, it is so that we may have faith to address that help innerly in our hearts and recognise the answers that are spoken there. We must do this, and I promise you that we shall not be disappointed.

NOVEMBER 1, 1955 There is always a chance and there is always help if we feel the need of them deeply enough. The only true helplessness is when man no longer feels the need of help.

NOVEMBER 20, 1955 How to escape from recurrence? By sacrificing one's unicellular 'liberty' and becoming absorbed into a higher organism with a higher aim. The single cell of an amoeba exists without any objective; a cell living in a human body shares its destiny.

The whole work of Ouspensky and Gurdjieff, and that which lies beyond it, is a cosmos, an organism formed in this present world for a spiritual purpose and a definite task. Real, genuine groups are the organs of this higher body; their individual members are its cells.

But what does it mean to be incorporated in this higher body? That is more difficult to answer. There are people who have attended meetings for ten years who have not become incorporated in it; there are others in some isolated place who do not personally know a single companion, yet who are completely integrated.

The direction of the work is spiritual. In order to respond to it, the soul has to grow and the vanity of personality has to shrink. All the work of preparation anticipates either the one or the other aspect of this change. What is the key to the process? It is to be sincere, to be honest, to be truthful. To be sincere means to find oneself, one's own way, one's own fate, without pretension, without imitation and without fear. To be honest means to pay one's debts to the extent that one can, in order to be able to be free to offer oneself to higher service without other obligation; to realise that everything that is good has its price that has to be paid by someone. To be truthful means little by little to abandon the subjective point of view based on likes and dislikes, and consider everything on the basis of objective laws, on divine truth. That is the preparation.

And the Work? The work is to give, to give in proportion to what one has, to give in proportion to what one understands. As an isolated cell, one can give nothing because one has nothing. As a cell already incorporated in a higher organism one can give all one wants to, certain that whatever one gives, one will recuperate from the unlimited reserves of the whole.

DECEMBER 22, 1955 More and more one part of the Work seems to me to be the making of contacts between people who at once recognise and understand each other. This true work is being done by many different kinds of people in many different guises and many different countries. But when they know each other independently of labels, it gives them more confidence and security in what they each have to do. The whole becomes more solid.

MARCH 11, 1956 To know the aim of others, it is necessary to help them. Help everyone, according to what they ask and need. By the kind of help they ask and their use of it, one will recognise their aim and they themselves will be able to recognise it. Ouspensky helped all who came to him—but he was so sincere and honest that only those who came through deep necessity dared approach him.

The more people come to us for help, the more we grow. They will ask for all kinds of help, but some will ask for spiritual help. And this will push us towards spiritual growth. This is the whole of the Work.

KAIROS, CHRONOS AND CROSSROADS

AUGUST 2, 1948 It seems to be arranged that fundamental change is only possible at very few moments in life—or death. But that what can happen in such moments is determined by the long gradual work of objective self-observation and understanding of natural laws. Without such preparation, these moments, if they occur, probably pass without recognition of their possibilities and everything remains exactly as before—as a train may pass over a set of points without the passengers even realising that there was an alternative line.

But with much observation, recognition of natural laws*, and self-remembering*, such moments, when they come, may yield very surprising understandings, perhaps even fundamental change. What is the nature of such moments is a different question—probably they enter all lives in one form or another. We cannot command them, but one day everything may depend on our previous preparation and attitude towards them.

JUNE 12, 1950 I think it is not for nothing that ancient religions like the Aztec or Mayan realised that for long cycles everything runs mechanically, but that at certain intervals between these cycles quite new possibilities exist and great efforts must be made. As far as I can see this does correspond with the structure of the universe in time.

AUGUST 7, 1951 I like very much indeed the distinction between *chronos* and *kairos*. This is something we need very much first to know about, and then to learn to sense. *Kairos* always connected with me with the law of octaves, and with becoming sensitive to the note which is sounding *now*. To be aware of the *kairos* for each action means evoking minimum resistance. Something which is quite easy to perform in its 'moment' may be impossible before, and terribly laborious afterward. To perform each thing in its own moment also means that it does not steal time from other things. I think the whole problem of how to make use of and enjoy all sides of life to the full is exactly connected with this question of the *kairos* for each thing and relationship, and with not allowing anything or any relation—however admirable—to steal from others. One must learn to feel what stars are shining. But most important of all, in our special work and in this time before us, becoming aware of the *kairos* means becoming aware of the great plan which is trying to realise itself *in its own time and in its own order.*

April 1, 1955 From time to time one reaches the point where the pressure of life seems almost unbearable. The important thing is to keep the flavour of the new and the longing for the miraculous in spite of everything. Sooner or later circumstances change, a crack opens in life and new possibilities again present themselves. But what enters at that moment depends exactly upon what one has been longing for during the time when nothing out of the ordinary was happening. We have spoken many times about crossroads in life. Between one crossroad and another one cannot change roads, only go on in the same direction. Shall we arrive at the next crossroads tomorrow, in six months or in five years? We do not know. We can only be ready to reach it at any moment.

August 1, 1953 The problem of crossroads is of the greatest interest. It is important to try to discover them in one's own past life. To look for the moments when the whole flavour of life changed, circumstances changed, friends and interests changed. From that comes the possibility of sensing the approach of new crossroads.

All the same, what interests me more is the idea of crossroads in the actual development of the great Work, in the growth of the force of the esoteric influence we know. For when a crossroads in the life of an individual coincides with another in the great Work, everything is possible. Without being able to define it, I feel in these months the approach of a crossroads on a big scale.

DECEMBER 24, 1953 We have to go on as best we can. Then when we come to a crossroads, things change according to what we have been feeling and working for during the dark time.

OCTOBER 24, 1954 At a certain point it was necessary to put all ordinary knowledge together as best one could, in the light of the tradition we have been given. But in a way this was and is only a preparation to receive *new knowledge, new help.* Only by assimilating all that ordinary life has to offer us, do we really qualify to receive direction from outside ordinary life. And yet at the same time this direction *is* available, for all who long for it. There is great work to be realised, and urgently. We all—individuals, groups, and even the whole of humanity—stand at a crossroads. At that crossroads we must appeal for help. For it is available, but only on condition that we demand it.

FEBRUARY 23, 1955 We are all at a crossroads. We become free only by affection, tolerance, understanding, self-remembering—there's no other way.

OCTOBER 3, 1955 I think we have come to a crossroads on many different scales. Some tremendous opportunity is preparing. But an opportunity is also a test, and the greater the opportunity the more drastic the sifting. Perhaps all our work is but preparation, so that as many as possible shall take advantage of that opportunity when it comes. The work now is the projection of harmony, on every scale, beginning with the achievement of harmony within oneself. The more harmony can be realised and understood, the more fully will this new opportunity be taken, and the more some parallel disaster will be diminished.

SUFFERING

SEPTEMBER 13, 1948 I am very interested in the idea of voluntary and involuntary suffering. First 'sacrifice your suffering'; only if a whole life is lived according to this principle does the idea of intentional suffering seem to become practical. I think it is almost impossible for those whose lives are full of involuntary suffering to be able to conceive of suffering as a positive thing. Their aim will always be and must be to escape suffering. At the same time this seems to me a very limited aim. I remember how it shocked me the first time I heard a certain person say that her aim was 'not to suffer'. Afterwards I saw that it could not be otherwise—because with all her strength she was so much at the mercy of involuntary suffering.

Suffering is a fixative—like the mordant used to fix a dye. It tends to fix whatever part of man's nature is uppermost while the suffering is being endured. Naturally, if it is involuntary it tends to bring with it resentment, self-pity and so on, and fixes them. On the other hand, if a man refuses to suffer except when he is making efforts for a definite aim and knows what he wants, then he tends to fix aim and determination. This is very useful.

MAY 5, 1949 If a man really begins to see that most of his suffering is unreal, if he begins to 'sacrifice his suffering', as it used to be said, then even in this life it loses its sting.

JULY 15, 1949 There is some inner mathematics of cause and effect which invisibly rules men's lives; and no real suffering is wasted. Only imaginary suffering is pure waste, leading nowhere. Real suffering is payment—for what, God knows, because we cannot remember what we owe—but payment of something which, sooner or later, must be paid. Only not to suffer more than is necessary, this is the thing. For to suffer mechanically, to begin to suffer by habit, is to start the whole chain again. If one can avoid that, then sooner or later the hard time must pass, and all kinds of new possibilities appear, which one may then at last—through hardship—be able to use.

Someone passes through your life and leaves an image that you cannot forget, nor find comfort from. But did you not leave such a trace in some other person's life, without caring or even knowing? Did I not, did not everyone? Everything must work itself out. All debts must be paid. All that one has inflicted one has to suffer, before one can become free. So those who wish for freedom can only say: Let what comes come: I will accept it.

It is not because I myself have any right to do so that I say this, but because I was shown that it is so. In Ouspensky's last months one saw how he accepted being old, sick, ugly, helpless, in pain, misunderstood, and indeed did everything to prevent others comforting him, to suffer consciously, to make it more difficult for him to be understood. For to be understood is what all men crave more than food, comfort, even life. And to sacrifice being understood by ordinary men in an ordinary way is both to become free, and to make possible a completely different understanding for those who desire it. From this utter acceptance of what had to come, from the endeavour to pay *more*, to suffer *willingly*, and to pay *in advance* of fate presenting the bill, Ouspensky became another man—and partly one saw how it was done.

So that while for ordinary people one can only wish to alleviate suffering as much as possible, to those who have become connected with this way of escape, one can only say: 'If you can suffer in the right way, it is good. If you can't, it doesn't matter.'

JANUARY 22, 1952 We need suffering. We all have to be purified. And suffering is the great purifier. Can we wish that it should not come, either to ourselves or to those for whom we wish growth and purification more than anything?

APRIL 22, 1952 We have to admit that unhappiness, painful experiences and even obvious mistakes can teach us much; and taken in the right way these same failures and discomforts can be the raw material of which understanding and will are made. The reconstruction of one's life does not of necessity mean that such difficulties must be avoided. On the contrary, it might imply that we faced the difficulties that in this life we avoided.

SEPTEMBER 10, 1952 I know that there is no way out of the treadmill of mental suffering in the constantly turning anguish of ordinary 'human' emotions. But if some old point of view about self can die, then the anguish can be transmuted into something utterly different. To me it would be the greatest hypocrisy to pretend that there is any way out while we live in old points of view, blaming others—whatever their sins—for that which takes place in our own hearts. When one has seen 'sacrificing one's suffering' produces miracles, one can no longer agree that it be cherished.

SEPTEMBER 24, 1952 It is very bitter to see inescapably that one has failed, when one knows that the incidents of sleep which ordinarily seem so small are not small at all, but determine our whole life. Sometimes one has to let the bitterness of failure sink in to the full and not try to save oneself from it.

At the same time I think it is very important to understand that this is our nature, we have all failed in this way, and will do so, being what we are. It is as though we have to swallow all that, accept others for what they are and ourselves for what we are and go on to a new place beyond both where we can look back on the world and ourselves with a kind of objective tolerance and affection. It is not on this level, in a put-up fight between one part of ourselves and another part that the solution lies, but in reaching some quiet place beyond where both sides look equally small and insignificant.

We were in the Cathedral in Florence. You come in at the main door and there are all the people, priests, choir boys, tourists, milling about on the ground level. There each one seems important to himself, and indeed he is. But then you painfully climb up a dark spiral stairway in the wall towards the dome, and at last come out in a gallery which runs round the inside of it. Suddenly, the whole church is spread out below you with all those tiny people indistinguishable one from another, and both you and they are equally lost in the great void which seems to make all one's previous thoughts disappear as pointless. Somehow this gallery seemed to mean knowledge of oneself as one is, full self-consciousness.

But when one had watched as much as one could bear to, one plunged into a hidden staircase which climbed to the top of the dome and at length emerged outside. Then there was the whole of Florence and the hills and woods and villages and distant scenery spread out below you under the sun and sky. All that one had seen and felt inside the cathedral, inside oneself, again disappeared in relation to the great universe. For this was reality, and the other only an image of it in stone! So that this lookout right under the cross suddenly seemed an image of true consciousness, objective consciousness of the world as it is, freedom.

JANUARY 26, 1953 Some difficulties are due to fears and prejudices dating back to many years ago, which lurk unresolved under the surface and at last come unescapably to the front. I now see very clearly that in each period of the Work certain lessons can and should be learned. If they are not learned, then they return far more forcibly in the next period, when in fact they provide the toughest resistance to change, because they are backed by will and determination which have been acquired by hard work. From this point of view, interesting and sobering to think of the lessons which we are failing to learn now and which will land with full force on the unsuspecting next generation. Indeed, a second series of difficulties seem exactly of this nature. They are connected with a tendency to take for granted proved conditions and to use them as a shield against the demands of life.

One calls these things difficulties. In fact they are precisely what makes changes and ascent possible. Without them we should all have gone to permanent sleep long ago.

SEPTEMBER 2, 1954 A teacher is held down by those who think he could have made no mistakes, and everything must be preserved exactly as he showed it. Those who love him more must take chances to help free him from the past, not mind if they look disloyal. There is no being who did not make mistakes, and who has not to do it better next time, better *now*.

I know that the Work is to make free men and brave men, who will work in any circumstances and apparently alone, secure in their inner connection and inner help. But how few of us want to be free or brave! This is why warnings about keeping away from harmful circumstances make me rather uneasy. They sound so reasonable, so right. But to avoid danger is so often to avoid opportunity, and he who successfully hides from the devil very often hides from God too. Men are naturally timid, and my experience is that they will eagerly snatch up such good advice to make their timidity decent.

The only answer I would wish to be able to give to: 'Quo Vadis?' is, 'Up!' That means constantly leaving more behind, constantly embracing a larger view. But how much help, how many kicks and cajolings we need to leave anything behind at all! Really I think it is the panorama alone that persuades us. And that is available for all to see—if they look round and up.

September 26, 1955 It seems one of the conditions of moving to another level, that one should feel and acknowledge that everything one has done on this one is utter failure in comparison with what should have been done. I think Ouspensky did really feel it and I know that he did pass to another level, where all is possible again.

December 9, 1955 When new tensions and forces begin to work in us they cause a very painful revolution in the depths of our being. For some, the greatest difficulty is to bear themselves and not get lost in remorse. But he who has learned not to take himself so seriously does not allow himself to become fascinated by his spiritual colic.

December 22, 1955 [The following was written to someone old and very ill.] The idea that you are coming to the end of your possibilities is a very great one. Think that the less you can do of yourself, the more God can do through you and to you. What you must find now is great faith, tremendous faith. There is no limit to what that will make possible. You have done everything you had to do in this life, your conscience is clean; what have you to worry about? Unlimited help is available, which for some of us is only prevented from reaching us in its fulness by our doubts of ourselves, our preoccupation with our own failings. We have to forget that, and find unselfish faith in the Hierarchy*, in the Work of God.

JANUARY 3, 1956 We must try to avoid both regret and blame, whether of others or of ourselves. They will lead us nowhere. There is much to be learned from what may seem to be a lost opportunity. Whether it was lost or not depends not upon what we did then but on how much understanding we can get out of it now. What looks to us like our mistakes can give us far more understanding than what we count as our successes.

MARCH 2, 1956 If one is pressed hard, it is so that one may find faith and become free. Our pasts are full of weak places, evasions, dishonesties, that we thought were buried and forgotten. But they have to come out. Sometimes it is very bitter. Now with this strong influence that is shining on us, all the flaws are appearing. Nothing can be hidden any more. Because everything has to be firm and solid under our work. So when we are hard-pressed, struggling with the consequences of the past, it is really proof that our work is strong and right. It means that we are being given a chance to go faster. If all the consequences of the past come to the surface it is so that we may face them and become free of them once and for all. And under great pressure one may find a faith one would never need at ease.

APRIL 1956 We all continually pass from sincerity to pretension, from pretension to remorse, from remorse to sincerity. We must observe the cycle, but not allow ourselves to be dis heartened by it. It is human nature. We accept it, trying to look at it from a higher, more objective, more impersonal point of view. To blame oneself too much is also to take oneself too seriously. No one remains discouraged by his own failures except he who was vain enough to believe himself above all failure.

April 6, 1956 Hold on—even though there seems nothing to hold to. Never give up hope—even though you do not know what you are hoping for. Hope and faith open all doors. If there is real suffering, people are purified by it. It is tremendously important that a number be purified.

DEATH

FEBRUARY 29, 1948 Whatever people may pretend, death is the central point. Some time it may be possible to tell the effect of being present at a conscious death—Ouspensky's. How this relieved one of the fear of death for good and made it possible to understand things about the meaning of death that are ordinarily beyond the power of man to understand. With the help of what was then shown, I think we can prepare for death and life in quite a different way.

SPRING 1948 Nothing is ever finally achieved till death, and even that must at the same time be merely a new beginning with new equipment.

NOVEMBER 1, 1949 I will try to tell you how I am.

I have to go back to the new beginning of everything for me—Mr Ouspensky's death. There is no other place to begin from, for me.

For he showed such things about death that one could never again be afraid of it, and still less of anything that might come in life. He showed it simply as the obverse of life, the harvest of what one feels and desires in life. At the same time he showed death as the greatest mystery, in which everything becomes possible, *nothing is impossible.*

And because he mastered death, extracted all possibilities from it as we looked on, he made a way open for other people, he made it not impossible for us to follow. So that in one way all one's life and everybody else's life was shown to be a preparation for finding all possibilities in death.

I know that read in a certain way this sounds strange, even morbid. But when one's relation to death is clear, then life, and every detail of life is filled with interest and sweetness in a way impossible before. And sometimes it seems that one only really lives when one is in right relation to death.

NOVEMBER 27, 1949 I think that Ouspensky knew very much

about death and what was possible in death long ago. In fact the introduction to *A New Model* shows that even then he had guessed something fundamental about it. But it was also his rule for himself that he only spoke of what he had experienced himself, what he could do and actually had done. And it seems to me that he deliberately kept back all he knew or guessed about death, until he should have died himself, proved to himself what possibilities it contained, and actually achieved them. Then in some way he could release into the understanding of those connected with him certain ideas he had deliberately withheld from them before, for lack of personal experience.

Now it seems that one can suppose death to contain all possibilities, all opportunities—but one's own power of realising possibilities, taking opportunities, will be neither greater nor less than it is now in life. Incalculable energy may be released in us at that moment, but our power of utilising it, riding it to the understanding and end we desire, will be just the same as our power of using the good energy our body gives us now. So I think that how one lives must create the way one dies.

JULY 11, 1950 Death is only interesting in relation to the search for what cannot die.

OCTOBER 31, 1950 I no longer feel it necessary to struggle in my mind against the idea of death—either other people's or my own—or to feel it so terrible. A life must come to an end, just as a cat's tail must. I wonder if it is really more terrible for it to happen today than in thirty years' time? Why should one have to look for some hidden reason in the one case and not in the other? It seems to me that death is its own reason, its own unanswerable argument. If we have to learn to accept life, as Ouspensky showed us those last weeks, surely we have to accept death too? And maybe, by not rebelling against it, it will begin to look different—not terrible at all, but full of other possibilities.

Yes, I know those who are left must suffer, seeing only what we see in our present state. And that is hard, both for them, and for those who love them. But can we ask the great laws of the universe to modify themselves to our so short sight, so little understanding? To me that is blasphemy. For myself I must ask to *see more*, on an even larger scale. And somehow that seems possible only by first *accepting*.

APRIL 19, 1951 All that lives must die, all that dies must be born again.

JUNE 7, 1951 In the whole demonstration which culminated in Ouspensky's death, perhaps the most extraordinary thing was that *nothing negative ever touched the idea of death*. I wish I could convey the realisation that in death there is *absolutely no need for fear*, even *no place for fear to exist*. For if one understands that one need not be afraid of this, then one knows that one need be afraid of nothing.

AUGUST 6, 1952 All our understanding of death is limited. In interpretations of death, one possibility does not exclude another. Every theory that man has been able to invent contains a certain element of truth, but none is the complete truth. Our task is to widen and widen our vision. Ouspensky's dying demonstration opened a door on to a wider panorama. And the door continues to be open.

SEPTEMBER 1954 Of course one can't be joyful over someone close to us passing into eternity—it is so far more mysterious, unknown and wonderful than we can imagine. But new chances it must mean, new beginnings, many new beginnings simultaneously perhaps.

NOVEMBER 2, 1955 At every death the doors between the worlds open for a while, and those who are sensitive may catch some indication through them.

THE NEW BEGINNING

JANUARY 23, 1948 Two currents begin to separate—those who see this new beginning, and through it quite new possibilities in a more free and individual way; and those who think that nothing new was shown, and who wish to perpetuate the old way and old attitudes. It must be like that. One has only to read the New Testament to see it was always so. And the only important thing, I believe, is that people of the two views should not fight or obstruct each other, but each go on with what they have to do.

MAY 1, 1949 There is much to say about Ouspensky's last months on earth. He returned to England in January 1947, a very ill man, but far from broken, a free one at last. I followed in April, stayed at Lyne, his house in the country, and was lucky enough to be with him all that summer. He held three or four big meetings in London in March, April and May, in which he spoke in quite a new way. He said: 'I abandon the System*', and refused to hear anything about its words or theory, forcing people to penetrate to what they really understood and wanted in their hearts. These meetings baffled some people, but made a very extraordinary impression.

Then he retired quietly to the country for the rest of the summer. He hardly spoke at all even to the people who were eating and sitting with him. Yet one had the sense that everything that was done was a kind of demonstration, and gradually an atmosphere developed which can hardly be described. Looking back, this seems the happiest and most vivid period of my life. He showed the few who were with him, without explanation, what it means for a man to pass consciously into the realm of the spirit.

He said that he was going back to America on September 4, and that we should make all preparations. We did so. On that day we went down to Southampton, put our luggage on board, and were ready to leave. A few hours before the boat was due to sail, he arrived at the dock, and suddenly said quietly, 'I am not going to America this time.' It was like the 'stop' exercise on the scale of the whole Work. A stop was made in many lives, everyone's personal plans were turned upside down, and a space made in the momentum of time where something quite new could be done.

Then a most extraordinary and indescribable time began. In the last month of his life, terribly weak and sick, he travelled all over the south of England to the places he had known, stayed up day and night, demanded more and more impossible tasks of himself, and seemed to rise in a crescendo of effort to meet the moment of death. During this time, many things which we call miraculous took place. In that month he made a new path for his people, and paid their debts for them. Then right at the end he said one strange morning, 'Now you must reconstruct *everything*, from the very beginning.' He died on October 2, 1947.

In the time before and since his death, for myself and many others, the whole idea and purpose of our work revealed itself in quite a different way. It became clear that before, we had taken everything in an extraordinarily flat, incomplete way. By demonstrating a conscious dying, Ouspensky seemed to show that in this lay all possibilities.

The meanings of reconstructing everything are unlimited. But in one meaning, it seemed the exact complement of his 'abandoning the system' of six months before. All must be given up, and then remade—both for each person, and for the system as a whole.

JUNE 1, 1949 People begin to feel that our ideas need all means of expression, and each person needs his own. Of course from each person's own point of view it looks as though he came to certain conclusions, certain understandings, himself. But when one sees many, many people—far apart and not in contact with each other—reaching the same point of view, it seems clear that it is a phase in the whole Work, a sort of unfolding of something at whose invisible beginning we were present.

So it sometimes seems that the whole thing now is to make and strengthen inner connections between all Ouspensky's people, and melt away any personal misunderstandings that prevent this, so that whatever great force wants to work through the whole may do so.

NOVEMBER 5, 1949 What Mr Ouspensky performed in his last days binds us all together and allows us to understand each other, through understanding him. It was of such power that every trace left by it must contain something of the same quality. One felt the happenings of another world very immediately, not as we usually suppose far away, but as *very close*, pervading us and everything, *creating something new*. In some way, Ouspensky forced the door between this world and another at that time—not only for himself, but for all those whose lives have become attached to his and who have positive attitude towards him. This is where everything is different from before, and where possibilities are open now which were not open—however much we tried—in the time before.

NOVEMBER 18, 1949 The new beginning for me was Ouspensky's death. Because I believe—I know—that at that time he actually achieved what we had all been talking about those many years, and in the process contacted very high school indeed.

The details are another story, a long extraordinary story, which to me contains all the indications we need to continue. I know that from an ordinary point of view all this sounds fantastic and superstitious. All I can say is that what we studied all those years never was ordinary, though in the end we began to persuade ourselves that it was. In fact, all that was explained about time*, and about higher levels of consciousness* bringing one to a completely different realm of time, with the power of moving through time and above time, contains the complete theory of Ouspensky's continued influence among us now and in the future. But the theory is for those who like it; it is the fact that alters everything.

For a practical programme—I base myself on the two chief 'practical' instructions of Ouspensky's last days. First, that he said: 'I abandon the system.' And second, that later he added: 'Now you must begin again from the beginning. Now you must reconstruct it all.' I take this to mean abandoning old forms, penetrating to the truth which lay behind those forms, and creating new forms for that truth—which in their turn must one day be abandoned also.

Abandoning and recreating seems to me the only way of keeping alive the hidden connection which lay behind the system. If one clings to the old, it fossilises, and oneself inside.

The idea of reconstruction seems to be endless. It will be different for each person according to his knowledge and capacity.

Reconstruction of the knowledge, its application to this field of research or that, its translation into scientific language, emotional language, artistic language, any language you like. But chiefly its reconstruction inside oneself, as the controlling principle of one's life. Which means reconstruction of one's life itself, past, present and future, in memory and in fact. And above all, reconstruction of one's relation with one's teacher, and all that follows from the line of his life crossing one's own.

FEBRUARY 22, 1950 It is very difficult to convey the strange springtime feeling of beginning from the beginning, of a new unspoiled start, which one gets in Mexico just now. Everything is growing, expanding, developing; everywhere building—houses, roads, factories, schools—and among all kinds of people an enormous enthusiasm, a sort of optimistic certainty in something, in some possibility. Only exactly what, nobody knows. But the sun shines, and the country is young, and life is cheap, and there are good things to come. Very often it reminds me of the England of the Canterbury Tales—the same fat new-rich burghers, clever and naive in equal proportions, the same eager idealistic young clerks, painters, writers, the same patient shrewd peasants, whose broad unshockable humour makes them wiser than anyone else.

For us the turn of the year seems to have brought a turn of emphasis. We seem to have met quantities of people, of so many different kinds, from politicos to ballet-dancers and miners. And with so many of them a kind of natural sympathy and understanding is possible. Only it becomes clear that one has to speak with each in his own language, take part in the actual life of each, before this natural link can develop further. It is very clear that things here cannot or should not be built on the formulation of an intellectual system—though it is also clear that many people are thirsty for ideas in a way they never can be in a highly educated country. But it is in actual life, in building, improving, educating, dancing, cultivating that the possibilities lie. And when ideas from a higher level come into this sweaty business of actual living in a country where everything has to be remade from the beginning, and can show a new way, or a new pattern, then people's interest and enthusiasm is almost startling. So we are learning, and we have to learn and learn to do everything differently.

MAY 4, 1952 I feel that one reason why it is important to travel is that one is able to go home and make a really new start. My experience is that it is almost impossible to begin anew simply by getting up and turning round in the same place. One has to step outside it for a moment, not only innerly, but also physically, I believe. Look at it and assess it from the outside. Then maybe one can return to it again and do what one has to do.

Sometimes we feel that a new beginning has been made, and that many old considerations, fears and irritations have been made unnecessary. Our heritage of psychological bad habits was quietly removed from our shoulders. But what seems to happen is that when the first flush of enthusiasm passes, out of sheer boredom or failure to see things in a new way, we begin once again to imitate our old reactions, not because we feel them but simply because they are more familiar than anything else. The trouble is that if we allow this to happen, quite soon we do begin to feel them and the whole vicious circle starts up once more. This is the past recapturing us again.

AUGUST 26, 1953 At the time of his death, Ouspensky created a new beginning on many different scales. In relation to oneself and one's own line of work one had some inkling of what this meant. The magnitude of the new beginning which lay behind one could hardly grasp. With every month or two it has seemed greater, until now one glimpses something world-wide and age-long. Perhaps Ouspensky's new beginning coincided with a greater new beginning on a cosmic scale.

About two months ago, the idea of harmony was suddenly dropped into our talk. Somebody remembered how at one of Ouspensky's last meetings the following interchange took place:

QUESTION: How can I find harmony?

OUSPENSKY: This is my question now, and I have no answer.

QUESTION: What does harmony mean?

OUSPENSKY: It is a musical term, nothing more.

When we looked up the word 'harmony' in the Oxford Concise Dictionary, we found a very interesting definition:

'HARMONY—Agreement; *pre-established h.* (between body and soul before their creation); agreeable effect of apt arrangement of parts; combination of simultaneous notes to form chords; sweet or melodious sound; collation of parallel narratives etc., especially of the four Gospels.'

We have thought a great deal about harmony. How the first requirement is that each of the notes created by the law of seven should sound clear and full and tone-perfect. Next these notes will be combined by the law of three to form major or minor chords or dischords. Finally these notes and chords may be harmoniously combined into music by a composer and player.

In the light of this the idea seemed to apply to every level of our work. In individual man, harmony among functions; harmony between body, soul and spirit; harmony among its different members, harmony between its leader and its origin; in the great esoteric impulse launched through Gurdjieff and Ouspensky, harmony among all lines and groups; harmony between them, their founders and God; in the world, harmony among all branches of knowledge, all peoples, all esoteric lines. Seen like this, it seemed quite clear why Ouspensky could say: 'This is my question now, and I have no answer.' The world being what it is, Christ Himself could say the same.

Was the new beginning for Gurdjieff and Ouspensky all part of the same great plan? The transfer of the two poles of the

Work from earth to a level where they could operate in an immensely more complete and penetrating way? I believe it is something like that. I believe that Great School, having an enormous new esoteric impulse to launch in the world, marked out two men who would act as opposite poles of this impulse and whose life work would be preparation for it. The real beginning, the conception of this new influence, I believe began with their deaths. Began when their polarity was translated to what we have come to call the electronic* world.

That was the conception. But when and what is the birth? Would not the whole effort be to create harmony, into which it could enter?

SEPTEMBER 9, 1954 One thing is clear. We must all go *on*. To new revelations, to new understanding, to new tasks, new responsibilities. I know that this going forward may often look strange and shocking at the time, as did Ouspensky's abandonment of the System. But we must do it. We must be melted down and remade, over and over again. We must pray that crystallisation does not overtake us.

FEBRUARY 7, 1955 Many people are waiting, expecting. They feel themselves on the edge of a new era, and they feel that quite new things are expected of them. But they don't know what. The weak ones lose themselves in imagination, fantasy and dreams, hoping that they will be carried into the new order floating on the tide, the strong ones work alone as best they can, and hope. They are waiting for this word of harmony. And they recognise it immediately.

AUGUST 16, 1955 We are moving into a new phase on a very big scale indeed. A change in influence far beyond the planets. We must never forget that we are passing into the new age. To play the part that we are prepared for, we have to belong to the future, and free ourselves from the past in every way. And we are working on a very long time-scale, whether we like it or not!

NOVEMBER 27, 1955 I am happy when people have the feeling

of a new beginning. Because it is like that for all those who allow themselves to be touched by this influence. There is so much to do in preparation for the future, so many different fields in which harmony must come, and all by means of ordinary everyday men like ourselves. The sooner one can get beyond the stage of personal preoccupation the better.

MARCH 5, 1956 A few people have to go forward. At the time of Ouspensky's death, I expressed it to myself that some had to 'break through'. Now it is the same.

CUZCO

PROBABLY the manner of each person's death is consistent with the manner of his life. Rodney had never spared himself physically, and in the last weeks, although suffering from an exhaustion that was obviously extreme, drove himself to hold daily meetings in Lima, innumerable private conversations and long hours of Movements. He admitted to feeling 'rather strange' in the high altitude of Cuzco—11,800 feet—and contrary to his life-long habit of avoiding medicines took several doses of coramine.

The day he arrived he found a cripple beggar-boy in the cathedral. After lunch, while the others in the party were resting, he took the boy up the mountain to the great statue of Christ that overlooks the town to pray that he might be healed. Then they went to the public baths where Rodney washed him with his bare hands and dried him with his own shirt. He then bought him new clothes. Outside the shop a crowd had gathered, intrigued that a foreigner should concern himself with a poor Indian boy. Rodney said to the crowd: 'This boy is your responsibility. He is yourselves. If you pray to Our Lord to make him well, he will be healed. You must learn what is harmony; you must learn to look after each other; you must learn to give—to give.' Someone in the crowd said: 'That's all very well for you—you're rich.' Rodney answered: 'Everyone can give something. Everyone can give a prayer. Even if you can't give anything else, you can always give a smile; that doesn't cost anything.'

That night a few people came to Rodney's room in the hotel to ask him about his work. During the conversation a man said: 'All my life I have wanted to pray, but have never been able to.' Rodney said: 'And what do you think you are doing now? What you just said, isn't that praying?'

Next day the boy came to take Rodney to the belfry of the cathedral to show him where he was allowed to sleep in a corner under the bells. To reach it there is a climb of ninety-eight steps. Afterwards Rodney went with the rest of the party to visit Inca ruins in the mountains.

After lunch, again while the others were resting, Rodney went out. He climbed up to the cathedral belfry to find the boy and sat on the step below the low containing wall, below an arch. He told the boy that he was going to arrange with a doctor to operate on his twisted leg. While talking he was looking at the statue of Christ on the mountain opposite. Suddenly he got up with a gasp as though his breath had failed, staggered forward onto the top of the low wall, grasping the two wooden beams that were supporting the arch. Then he fell forward, striking his head against one of them. His body fell onto the wide cornice that juts out below and slipped off, falling to the street below. He lay where he fell, his arms out sideways in the form of a cross, his eyes open as though looking up at the sky, smiling.

It is not unusual for a man to die of a heart attack after climbing a long flight of steep stairs at such an altitude after weeks of physical effort in a state of exhaustion. It is the natural consequence of physical conditions. It is also natural, on a different level, for a man who has believed with all his being that the object of life is to give all he has for the love of God, in the end to give himself.

On his tomb in the cemetery in Cuzco are engraved the words he wrote two months before his death:

I was in the presence of God;
I was sent to earth;
My wings were taken;
My body entered matter;
My soul was caught by matter;
The earth sucked me down;
I came to rest.

I am inert;
Longing arises;
I gather my strength;
Will is born;
I receive and meditate;
I adore the Trinity;
I am in the presence of God.

QUESTIONNAIRE

In January 1955 Rodney was sent a questionnaire by an Argentinian journalist. Here are the questions and his answers, with his prefatory comment.

> It must be understood that these questions cannot be answered simply by verbal formulas. It needs many years of special study and experiment even to understand the meaning of the words that have been used. A game of chess with ideas, that leaves being and consciousness just as before, is quite useless. So the comments on the questions should not be taken as answers, but only as an indication of the long work necessary for each individual to come to his own conclusion.

1. *Your teaching—those of you who follow Peter Ouspensky—has it the clarity and emotional force necessary to interest the mass of people who are hungry for spiritual things?*

It is the work of conscious harmony. Who does not long to live in harmony?

2. *Your school says that an individual must find himself, feel himself an integral part of humanity, remember what he was, is and will be, and that to do this he must become conscious of his three bodies. How can this be explained so that simple people will understand it?*

Wake up and live. Feel yourself a living being, among living companions, enveloped in the living God. That means, be real, be your whole self. Remember who you are.

3. *What meaning has the new era for you? What is it bringing to the world, and how should man receive it?*

In other periods, in isolated areas, among isolated races, through isolated religions, there were ways by which some sides of man could be developed at the expense of others. Today isolation is impossible. Everything exists everywhere. We share all history, all the universe, the achievements of all races, sciences and religions. The new era has to reconcile all this, achieve a vision of the harmonious whole.

4. *Do you think that we are on the eve of some great and strange event? What could it be and what is its meaning?*

At the beginning of every age Great School, the Inner Circle of Humanity, the Church Triumphant, produces a physical drama on the earth to demonstrate man's next task. The last complete production was that of Christ, described in the Gospels. Another is approaching.

5. *Could it be that this event is connected with the coming of a World Teacher, who will bring us the help needed to save us from the chaos in which we are?*

God willing.

6. *Where is our planet and its inhabitants going? What kind of changes in civilisation do you think will come?*

Our planet is growing up. It is time to leave childish things.

7. *Do you believe in the reality of cosmic forces which can be invoked and used to improve the state of the world and of individuals? How to appeal to them? And how to receive them?*

Every minute we are enveloped, bathed, in such forces, from the living magnetism of the planets to the love of God Himself. How to appeal to them? By doing one's whole duty. How to receive them? By making silence in the heart, and listening.

8. *How can the universal brotherhood, which is so much desired by all good men, be hastened and brought about?*

Outside our time and space, where Great School works, this universal brotherhood already exists. They are trying to project it into our time and space. If we appeal to that place beyond time, we feel it, we receive it. Universal brotherhood can only be felt in the remembrance of eternity. By remembering oneself in eternity.

9. *Do you believe that there is some new and revolutionary system by which people can be prepared for all events, spiritual, astral and geological?*

There *is* a universal key. It must first be found, then studied, and finally used. But what is the door you want to open?

10. *Can nuclear energy and the hydrogen bomb destroy mankind and the planet? Or could it be transformed for the good of men?*

When a new gift, a new possibility, is given to the earth, it is always presented in two ways—in unconscious form, and in conscious form. In the hydrogen bomb we recognise the unconscious form of a power hitherto unknown on earth. We await the demonstration of the same power in conscious form, that is, incarnate in living beings.

11. *Do you think that prayer is scientifically adequate to give us faith and strength in our aims?*

There is prayer of the flesh, which longs for satisfaction, prayer of the limbs in sacred dances, prayer of the mind in verbal formulas, prayer of the heart which loves God, and simultaneous prayer of all functions, of the whole being. He who knows how to pray with his whole being can never doubt.

12. *Are faith, hope, charity and love utopian, or are they paths which lead us to our highest possibilities?*

Faith begins by never doubting a truth we have once recognised. Hope begins by not taking ourselves too seriously. Charity begins by smiling at our neighbour. Love begins in two ways—by remembering ourselves, and by forgetting ourselves.

13. *We are at a crucial point. Should man go on studying, filling himself with knowledge? Or should he devote himself to his fellows, relieve human suffering as much as he can?*

Why not both things? And the third which reconciles them is to give oneself to God. Begin at any point you like, but go on till you complete the triad.

14. *Many people are appearing who seem to bring important gifts to mankind, faith healers, healers by prayer, by magnetism, by cosmic fluid and so on. Do you think these forces are really sound?*

Faith is and always has been the basis of all healing. The more the world prepares to recognise One Who must come, the more false prophets will arise to test its judgement.

15. *Do you think the coming of the flying saucers has anything to do with the new age?* 16. *Do you think men will learn from them about interplanetary travel?*

The Solar System is a cosmos as the human body is a cosmos. The planets are organs of that celestial body. Think in how many ways the organs of the human body communicate with each other. By the bloodstream, by the lymph, and by various nervous systems. When man awakes consciously a new nervous system of communication comes into play. If the Solar System is reaching a new stage of consciousness, there should be a new form of communication between the planets.

17. *What will science do, in face of flying saucers and other supernatural phenomena?*

The first-class scientists are extending the field of human understanding in an extraordinary way. The science of today is not the science of fifty years ago nor even of ten.

18. *What kind of progress could our civilisation expect if there were an intelligent union of science, religion, philosophy and art?*

We just have to go on living for a few more decades, and then we'll see.

19. *What do you think about the prophecies of the Great Pyramid about the period beginning August* 20, 1953?

I don't know. On August 20, 1953, I was making a bonfire of all my old papers.

20. *What is this one directing hierarchy behind all the constructive movements of the new era?*

It is made up of Christ and His Saints, though of course they are known by different names in different parts of the world.

21. *How can we help to realise the new era, the reconstruction of the world, ourselves and our consciousness?*

Be sincere—that is, find yourself. Be honest—that is, pay your debts. Be truthful—that is, leave your egoism and live through understanding of universal laws.

22. *Do you think the federation of all spiritual movements is necessary to prepare for the coming of a World Teacher? Or do you think they should be merged into one?* 23. *What do you think of all these spiritual movements?*

Recognise your companions on the way, no matter what name they go by. Recognise sincerity, kindness, truth, no matter who expresses it. Recognise that spiritual unity already exists—outside time and space. Work and pray. The rest will come by itself.

24. *Do you believe that people today should try more than ever to perceive harmony between man, the world, nature, his fellows, the stars and God?*

It is the work of conscious harmony. Who does not long to live in harmony?

NOTES EXPLAINING THE SPECIAL WORDS USED IN THE LETTERS

ACTIVITIES — See note on Processes

BODY — See note on Molecular

BUFFERS — Just as free circulation of blood throughout the body is necessary for physical health and growth, so free circulation of memory throughout the long body of man's life is necessary for health and growth of essence. Where blood-circulation fails, where organs are blocked or constricted against its flow, there disease inevitably strikes. So also in the temporal sequence of life. Those years, months, incidents or relationships which we do not wish to remember begin to fester for lack of understanding. A blockage forms, a 'complex' develops, and without our recognising what is happening, the whole present may become poisoned *by that which we will not remember.*

. . . Loss of memory cannot be corrected by any mechanical method or treatment, but only consciously, by will and understanding.

The Theory of Celestial Influence, p. 218

CENTRES — See note on Functions

CONSCIOUSNESS — See note on Man, Higher level of

COSMOS — The word *kosmos* in Greek means 'order', 'harmony', 'right behaviour', 'honour', 'a whole', 'the outward fashion of a whole', and finally 'the harmonious order of the whole', 'the universe in its perfection'. As used by the Pythagoreans it also meant 'a self-evolving or self-transcending whole'. As we shall see in detail later, the possibility of self-evolution or self-transcendence implies a very special plan and structure which some creatures have and others do not have. Thus man, who possesses the possibility of perfecting and transcending himself, can be called a cosmos, whereas a dog, which seems to be a finished experiment with no further possibilities, cannot. By the same token, a sex-cell, which can transcend itself into a man, is probably a complete cosmos, whereas a bone-cell is not; a planet, which can transcend itself into a sun, is a complete cosmos, whereas an asteroid is not, and so on.

The token of a true cosmos is in fact a particular kind of design, referred to in the Book of Genesis in the phrase 'God created man *in his own image*'. This 'divine image', the characteristics of which we must study in detail, can be found on all levels, and is the hallmark of a cosmos. *Ibid, p. 17*

A man is a cosmos, whose times and perceptions bear a definite cosmic relationship to the times and perceptions of lesser and greater cosmoses. *Ibid, pp. 87, 88*

DIMENSIONS

Each cosmos may be considered as having six dimensions, three of space and three of time. These dimensions are exactly but differently related to the six dimensions of all other cosmoses. Line, surface, space, time and eternity are thus appearances which slide one into the other according to the scale of perception of the beholder. *Ibid, p. 25.* After his death a note was found among R's papers correcting his previous ideas on dimensions. 'We live in three dimensions—matter, space and time. Space and time can each be divided into three factors. Of the space-dimension the first, second and third factors are length breadth and thickness. Of the time-dimension the first factor is individual life-time; the second, the recurrence of this time, that is, all existing life-times taken as a whole; the third, all life-times, past, present and future, taken as a whole. Here again we find the combination of the laws of Three and Seven —three dimensions divided into seven factors. For weight, mass and density are but different ways of expressing the ponderability of matter and cannot be divided into separate factors. So there are three factors of space, three of time and one of matter, making seven in all. These are the dimensions in which we live, by which we are bound, "Maya". The Fourth Dimension, interpenetrating the other three, is reality. "*Unity exists*", as Ouspensky exclaimed in the Introduction to *A New Model*—those strange and ecstatic paragraphs that we so long ignored because we had not yet the experience to enable us to understand them'.

ELECTRONIC — See note on Molecular

ENNEAGRAM — Literally 'figure of nine', described by P. D. Ouspensky in *In Search of the Miraculous* as 'a certain symbol' which 'points out a method of cognising the essential nature of a thing examined in itself'.

ESSENCE — See note on Personality

FAKIR — Asceticism . . . This is the way of achieving consciousness by mastering physical functions, *by overcoming pain.* It is the way of transmuting pain into will. In the East it includes many fakir practices, and in its full form is known as hatha yoga. *Ibid, p.* 237

Food of Interior Impressions

Man lives and develops by the parallel assimilation of food, air and perceptions.

Ibid, p. 161

In the case of perceptions, particularly, digestion is not automatic, is not assured by nature at all. *It depends entirely on the degree of consciousness of the receiver.* And with increase in this consciousness, perceptions may be refined to a point where they give rise to degrees of ecstasy ordinarily unimaginable by us. *Ibid, p. 179*

When a man really absorbs something and understands it, it enters into him and becomes part of him . . . perceptions of greater worlds, greater forces, higher ideals, higher possibilities, . . . will nourish and enrich essence.

Ibid, p. 209

Such growth of essence . . . will imply a change of the whole being of man, an inner accumulation of energy and force.

The possibility of higher states of consciousness in man precisely depends upon certain fine matters produced by the body being subject to his *attention*. *Ibid, p. 210*

Forces

See note on Three

Functions

Functions (Listed on p. 5 of *The Theory of Eternal Life* as digestion, motion, respiration, instinctive-metabolism, thought, passionate emotion, creative or sex; and in a lecture in 1955 as intuition, digestion, movement-breathing, blood circulation, thought, projection and reproduction. Ed.)

Besides the languages recognisable by man through his ordinary functions, there are other forms of language arising from and appealing to supernormal functions, that is, functions which can be developed in man, but which he does not ordinarily enjoy. For instance, there is the language of higher emotional function, where one formulation has the power of conveying an enormous number of meanings—either simultaneously or in succession. Some of the finest poetry, which can never be exhausted, and which, though it always yields something fresh, can never be fully understood, may belong to this category. More evidently, the Gospels are written in such language, and for this reason their every verse can convey to a hundred men *a hundred different but never contradictory meanings.*

In the language of higher emotional function, and particularly of higher intellectual function, symbols play a very large part. For symbols are based on an understanding of true analogies between a greater cosmos and a smaller, a form or function or law in one cosmos being used to hint at the corresponding forms, functions and laws in other cosmoses. This understanding belongs exclusively to higher or potential functions in man, and must always produce a sense of bafflement and even frustration when approached by ordinary functions, such as that of logical thought. *Ibid, p. XIII*

GEOFF (Geoffrey Holme, a member of the group in Mexico, who died on December 12, 1954. Ed.)

HIERARCHY There exists an invisible Hierarchy of spirits who order and direct all the different aspects of life on earth and of humanity. That which Ouspensky calls the Inner Circle of Humanity, that which the Church calls the Church Triumphant, that is what we call the Hierarchy.

The Hierarchy consists in Our Lord Jesus

Christ, the spirit and redeemer of our universe, and all His conscious helpers, great and small. This Hierarchy, according to our tradition, has always projected and been the impulse behind the civilisation of the earth.

From a lecture delivered by Rodney Collin *in Mexico January 12, 1956*

Hydrogen

In our discussion of the universe, one of the chief purposes has been to discover the relative density of different worlds or phenomena. For it may be supposed that less dense means also more powerful, more penetrating, wider-ranging, more intelligent . . . the process of growth, by which we believe the whole universe to have been created, could be described by the formula: the descent of spirit into matter, and its endowment with form. Differing densities may then be seen as differing proportions of matter and spirit in the substances of worlds under consideration . . . The intention . . . is to establish some kind of measuring-scale, which would be capable of measuring all beings and forces from the Absolute to the Abyss.

The Theory of Celestial Influence, p. 93

All things, *all* influence, *all* life, matter and form may be regarded as emanating from the Sun in the fulness and totality of time.

. . . for perhaps three billion years the Sun has poured its immense and unvarying force into the substance of its planets and into the empty space between . . . what is the source of such immense and constant energy, and what is its nature? *Ibid, p. 68*

The active element in the Sun is hydrogen.

Ibid, p. 70

The transformation of hydrogen into light represents a *change of matter into a state in which it can be transmitted at long distance . . .* Hydrogen is, so to speak, the matter of suns, the fuel from which they create the radiations necessary to transmit life to their systems.

Ibid, p. 71

Atoms . . . consist of a central nucleus round which revolves a number of electrons, varying with the element concerned. The simplest atom is that of hydrogen, which has one electron. *Ibid, p. 69*

As hydrogen possesses the lowest atomic weight of all the elements, its atomic weight was formerly adopted by chemists as unity, and those of other elements were referred to it . . . The atomic number of hydrogen is 1.

Chambers' Encyclopedia

The table of quanta of radiant energy, the table of atomic weights of elements, and the table of molecular weights of compounds, do in fact form one single scale, extending from heaven to hell, and on the different rungs of which are to be found every substance knowable and unknowable. From this point of view everything may be regarded as physical and everything as comparable. The free motion of electrons which reaches the earth from the sun represents the highest and most rarefied form of physical matter which we know; the greater the colonies of such electrons locked together by the earth, the denser the substance derived therefrom . . .

The Theory of Celestial Influence, pp. 99-100

I's — In the ordinary way, there is neither permanence nor consciousness in man. Each of his functions speaks in him, automatically and in turn, with a different voice, for its own interests, indifferent to the interests of the others or of the whole, yet using the tongue and the name of the individual.

'I must read the paper!' intellectual function says.

'I'll go riding!' motor function contradicts.

'I'm hungry!' declares digestion.

'I'm cold!' metabolism.

And 'I'll not be thwarted!' cries passionate emotion, in the defence of any of them. Such are the many I's of man.

The Theory of Eternal Life, p. 7

IMMORTAL

It is the cellular body whose time begins with conception and terminates at death. But . . . from man's point of view, molecular and electronic time not only exist *within* his physical body, but also *after* it and *before* it. Thus molecular and electronic time, with all they imply, must be closely connected with the problem of states after death and before birth.

It is the penalty of man's feeble awareness, which cannot normally escape from the time and form of his cellular body, that this immortality of molecular and electronic matter does not concern him. But were he to create for himself a consciousness sufficiently powerful to penetrate into those other worlds and times which are contained within his own familiar body, then his whole relation to immortality might indeed be different.

The Theory of Celestial Influence, p. 171

Conscious immortality is connected with the power of passing freely from one form to another, of transcending lower forms for higher. It is the quality of a life-principle which has become independent of dying forms. *The Theory of Eternal Life, p. 103*

INTERVAL

See note on Octave

LAWS Man has two ways of studying the universe. The first is by induction: he examines phenomena, classifies them, and attempts to infer laws and principles from them. This is the method generally used by science. The second is by deduction: having perceived or had revealed or discovered certain laws and principles, he attempts to deduce the application of these laws in various specialised studies and in life. This is the method generally used by religion. The first method begins with 'facts' and attempts to reach 'laws'. The second method begins with 'laws' and attempts to reach 'facts'.

These two methods belong to the working of different human functions. The first is the method of the ordinary logical mind, which is permanently available to us. The second derives from a potential function in man, which is ordinarily inactive for lack of nervous energy of sufficient intensity, and which we may call higher mental function. This function, on the rare occasions of its operation, reveals to man *laws in action*, he sees the whole phenomenal world as the *product of laws*. *The Theory of Celestial Influence*, *p. xv*

LEVELS See note on Man, Higher level of

MAN, HIGHER LEVEL OF Man has the possibility of re-creating himself, or more correctly, the human being has the possibility of making itself into a man . . . what distinguishes man from animals is his possibility of becoming conscious of his own existence and of his place in the universe.

Ibid, *p. 198*

We have a basis for classifying men according to their degree of consciousness. First, there is the enormous mass of ordinary men in whom consciousness, if it exists at all, only occurs momentarily and by accident. Second, there are those for whom the idea of consciousness has penetrated into essence, and thus acquired duration and reliability. And finally, there is a small handful of men, scattered through history and across the world . . . for whom self-consciousness is permanent. The true history of humanity is the history of the influence of these conscious men. *Ibid, pp. 220-221*

MIRACLE

Someone must produce a play *in life.* The plot of the drama, its chief event, will be *the death of the producer* . . . and all the miraculous events and manifestations which follow his death may in one sense be seen as a demonstration that *the play has succeeded,* the tremendous miracle has been accomplished . . . A crack has been produced through all levels of matter and through time itself by the direct intervention of electronic energy. Through this crack the perception of ordinary men may for a short time see into higher worlds . . . And through it, for all beings, there now lies a way of escape which did not exist before.

The Theory of Eternal Life, pp. 108, 112, 113

After this, Ouspensky . . . demonstrated that change of consciousness the theory of which he had explained so many years.

The Theory of Celestial Influence, p. xxi

MOLECULAR

Any process of improvement or regeneration of natural or human forms must consist in unlocking more and more of the matter of the body from mineral first into molecular and then into electronic state. *Ibid, p. 62*

In man, the second state is connected with the development of a new *molecular* body, capable of assimilating the consciousness of another, and the third with the creation of a further *electronic* body, capable of generating its own consciousness and embracing others within it. Elsewhere we shall speak of these potential new bodies as the soul and spirit.

Ibid, pp. 201, 202

MOVEMENTS — Actual dances brought from the East, and reconstructed some years since in Europe and America. These dances have not only a symbolic but practical effect both on performers and on audience.

Preface to Hellas, published by the Stourton Press, Cape Town, 1951

OCTAVES — The octave or musical scale is a notation, adapted to man's hearing, of . . . a great law which controls the development of all processes in the universe.

The Theory of Celestial Influence, p. 81

PERSONALITY — Personality—in a right and useful sense—from the Latin 'persona', a player's mask, that through which the actor speaks. Right personality stands between the essence of man and the outside world. It is his psychological 'skin', his protection from life and means of adjusting to it. It includes all that he has learned about orientating his organism among his surroundings, the way he has learned to speak, think, walk, behave and so on, all his acquired habits and idiosyncrasies. Only in ordinary man this adaptation to life, this savoir faire which enables him to protect his inner life from unnecessary shocks and distractions, is so inextricably mixed with pretence and invented attitudes, that the two are quite inseparable. We have to take them as one phenomenon, as personality, which even at its best is something unreal, without material substance. *Ibid, p. 206*

Processes The principle that six cosmic processes, universally applicable, must result from the interaction of three forces was fully recognised by seventeenth century alchemy, whose theory and practice was based on the six alchemical operations—coagulation, dissolution, sublimation, putrefaction, separation and transmutation—resulting from different reactions of salt, sulphur and mercury.

The Theory of Celestial Influence, p. 53

Wherever three forces interact, they can manifest in six different combinations or orders. *Ibid, p. 154*

Growth, digestion (or refinement), elimination (destruction), corruption, healing, regeneration. *Ibid, p. VIII*

Real I See note on Personality

School . . . some men would actually succeed in becoming regenerated, in being transformed or transfigured into new beings. About these, however, it is difficult to tell, because very often—though not always—by their very transfiguration they disappear out of the ordinary course of history and are no more seen.

Certain traces of their existence may be left, however. Once they have succeeded in becoming regenerated or transformed their work will be in organising 'schools of regeneration', whose inner work must remain unseen. But such schools may also have engaged in some external expression of their work, such as the building of temples, the writing of scriptures, the conduct of scientific research, and so on. *Ibid, p. 314*

Self-Remembering . . . the potentiality which exists in man, of becoming conscious of his own existence and of his relation to the surrounding universe.

Ibid, p. 207

Self-remembering enables a man *to be himself.*

Ibid, p. 208

No phenomenon is produced by two forces; every phenomenon and every real result requires three forces. The practice of self-remembering or division of attention (between oneself and one's surroundings) is connected with the attempt to produce a certain phenomenon, the birth of consciousness in oneself. And when this begins to happen, attention recognises with relief and joy not two but three factors—one's own organism; . . . the situation to which this organism is exposed in the moment; and something permanent which stands on a higher level than both and which alone can resolve the relation between the two.

What is this third factor which must be remembered? Each person must find it for himself, and his own form of it—his school, his teacher, his purpose, the principles he has learned, the sun, some higher power in the universe, God.

The Theory of Celestial Influence, p. 215

SEVEN — See note on Octaves

SHOCK — As when a match is struck, intense friction is necessary in order to produce light.

Ibid, p. 328

SPEEDS OF FUNCTIONS — What is the actual relation between the three nervous systems? In the first place we must suppose them working with three different energies at three different speeds. The slowest is the cerebro-spinal system, which can only work as fast as we can think. Next faster is the sympathetic system, which enables the complicated instinctive processes of digestion, tissue-building and so on, to be carried on much faster than we can follow. While fastest of all should be the parasympathetic, or vagus system, which carries the immeasurably rapid impulses of intuition, self-preservation and sex. *Ibid. pp. 153, 154*

SUN, FOOD FOR

If the whole universe eats and is eaten, what then eats man? The answer appears to be, something higher than the earth. That which is of next higher nature above the earth and planets is the sun. The sun should eat man. But we know that men's corpses . . . are eaten by the earth . . . What then could it mean that men should be eaten by the sun? It can only refer to that part of man which distinguishes him from all other vertebrates, that is, his consciousness.

The Theory of Celestial Influence, pp. 126, 127

SYSTEM, THE

An extraordinary system of knowledge said to be a very ancient one, which had always existed in hidden form and traces of which could from time to time be seen coming to the surface of history in one guise or another. Although it explained in an extraordinary way countless things about man and the universe . . . its sole purpose was to help individual men *to awake to a different level of consciousness.* . . . In the bitter early spring of 1947 Ouspensky called several large meetings in London . . . He said that he abandoned the system . . . But at dawn one September day a fortnight before his death, he said: 'You must start again. You must make a new beginning. You must reconstruct everything for yourselves.'

This then was the true meaning of 'abandoning the system'. Every system of truth must be abandoned, in order that it may grow again. *Ibid, pp. xviii, xx, xxi*

Three According to many ancient systems of philosophy, all phenomena that exist arise from the interaction of three forces. One is described as of an active or creative nature; the second as passive or material; and the third as mediating or formative

. . . The characteristics of the three forces depend, not upon the phenomena through which they manifest, but upon their relation to each other. *Ibid, pp. 49, 50*

Time, Outside Our sense of time derives from the physiological unfolding of the body . . . The cellular body is our clock . . . The shock which destroys it frees us from time.

At death we enter timelessness or eternity. From that state of timelessness . . . all points within time are equally accessible.

The Theory of Eternal Life, p. 9

Types The glands, in the order of their distance from the heart, obey the same laws as the planets in the order of their distance from the sun. Created from the same design, the one responds to the other.

We now have a basis for studying the possibility of planets ruling different organs, and by extension the types which these receptive organs dominate.

Man was believed to contain within him *all* affinities, and these separate affinities were established in different organs and parts . . . From this it followed that a man who had one organ or part highly developed, whose centre of gravity lay there, so to speak, enjoyed a special affinity or sensitiveness for the corresponding planet. He was of that *type*.

The Theory of Celestial Influence, pp. 142, 143

At the same time, it must be remembered that

there are no such things as pure types, for in every man *all* the glands must function . . . Moreover, every gland affects and is affected by every other, so that in practice it is impossible to 'isolate' the effect of any.
. . . In a 'perfect' man the action of the glands would be exactly balanced, and the nearer a man approaches this balance, the less is it possible to classify him as a type.

Ibid, p. 147

WAY

The soul of a civilisation is fed in three ways —those three traditional ways by which men may become conscious . . . These 'ways', and the schools of regeneration which exist to administer them and teach their methods on earth, depend upon the idea of developing consciousness first in one particular function. By becoming fully conscious in one function, a man finds his way to consciousness of his whole being.
The first way to consciousness is through the instinctive and motor functions. The second way is through the emotional function. The third is through the intellectual function.
The first way is something akin to what in the west is known as *asceticism* . . .
The second way depends on a marriage of what are known in the west as *mysticism* and *charity*, though both words are unsatisfactory. It is the way of achieving consciousness by mastering the emotional function, *by overcoming fear*. It is the way of transmuting fear into love. *Ibid, pp. 237, 238*
The third way is what used to be understood by *philosophy*. It is the way of transmuting thought into understanding.
There is, however, a fourth way . . . It consists in mastering instinctive, emotional and

intellectual functions *at the same time*; in transmuting pain, fear and thought into their higher counterparts of will, love and understanding *simultaneously* . . .

The fourth way is carried out in the conditions of ordinary life . . . It will be *that which lights up all that happens.*

Schools of the fourth way have existed and exist, just as schools of the three traditional ways existed and exist. But they are much more difficult to detect, because—unlike the others—they cannot be recognised by any one practice, one method, one task, or one name.

The Theory of Celestial Influence, pp. 239, 240, 241

WHIRLING ECSTASY, THE

March 21, 1955 The Whirling Ecstasy

This booklet (published by Ediciones Sol, Mexico) is a selection from *The Lives of the Gnostics* by Aflaki, disciple of Jellal-ed-din Rumi's grandson, written between 1318 and 1335. It was translated into French by C. Huart under the title *Les Saints des Dervisches Tourneurs* (Paris 1918-22) and from French into English by Rodney Collin in 1944.

WORLDS, HIGHER

See note on Miracle